Walks
1066
Country
By
Nick Brown

publications

First published in Great Britain in 2010 by Trailguides Limited.
www.trailguides.co.uk

ISBN 978-1-905444-39-7

Trailguides Limited
35 Carmel Road South
Darlington
Co Durham DL3 8DQ

Cover design by Steve Gustard

Printed in Great Britain by the MPG Books Group, Bodmin and King's Lynn

CONTENTS

Page

INTRODUCTION

1. Introduction to the 1066 Area   4
2. The Walks   4
3. The Maps   6
4. Tourist Information Centres & Websites   6
5. Accommodation   7
6. The Countryside Code   7

THE WALKS

Walk 1. Herstmonceux	4.20 miles.	9
Walk 2. Steven's Crouch	6.70 miles.	15
Walk 3. Battle	4.20 miles.	21
Walk 4. Crowhurst	8.50 miles.	27
Walk 5 North's Seat	6.80 miles.	33
Walk 6. Pett Level	6.25 miles.	39
Walk 7. Guestling	7.00 miles.	44
Walk 8. Icklesham	3.90 miles.	50
Walk 9. Camber Castle	5.75 miles.	55
Walk 10. Rye	8.40 miles.	62
Walk 11.Northiam	3.33 miles.	69
Walk 12.Bodiam	5.75 miles.	74
Walk 13.Brede	5.85 miles.	81
Walk 14.Sedlescombe	6.10 miles.	88

APPENDIX

The Author	94
Walking South East	95
Acknowledgements	96
Disclaimer	96

INTRODUCTION

1. Introduction to the 1066 area

A selection of 14 superb routes for walkers and dog walkers in the 1066 area, which is famed for its stunning diversity of scenery and wealth of local history. These include the picturesque towns of Battle and Rye, the impressive castles of Bodiam and Herstmonceux, the cliff top path at Fairlight Cove, the glorious gardens at Great Dixter in Northiam, and countless Anglo-Saxon and Norman churches!

Many of the routes incorporate sections of the 1066 Country Walk, which is 31 miles long. It starts at Pevensey in East Sussex where William the Conqueror landed in 1066 and goes via Battle, where he defeated King Harold at the Battle of Hastings, and finishes at Rye. Several routes also take in sections of the Sussex Border Path with Kent.

There are also many relatively "undiscovered" routes which will enable you to enjoy this magnificent countryside at its best! These include the Brede and Tillingham Valleys, Rye Harbour Nature Reserve and the Royal Military Canal at Pett. Superb photos accompany each route, together with easy to follow hand-drawn maps and interesting snippets of local history. Routes vary from 3.33 miles to 8.50 miles and are graded for degree of difficulty.

For each booklet sold, 30% of the author's profits will go directly to St. Michael's Hospice in Hastings. The hospice cares for 400 patients as well as making 2300 hospice visits at home each year. The current running costs are £5 million per annum, of which only £1.8 million comes from NHS grants and nursing home fees, so the hospice relies heavily on donations and sponsored events. For more details please visit their website www.stmichaelshospice.org .

2. The Walks

- All walks are easily accessed within a maximum 20 minute drive from Hastings
- Wide variety of 14 walks, ranging from 3.33 to 8.50 miles in distance
- Walks are graded for degree of difficulty, ranging from 1 (EASY) to 5 (VERY TESTING !)
- Dog walkers are advised on each route as to the likelihood of encountering sheep and cows
- Superb photos accompany each route; additional photos can be accessed on **www.spanglefish.com/1066routes**

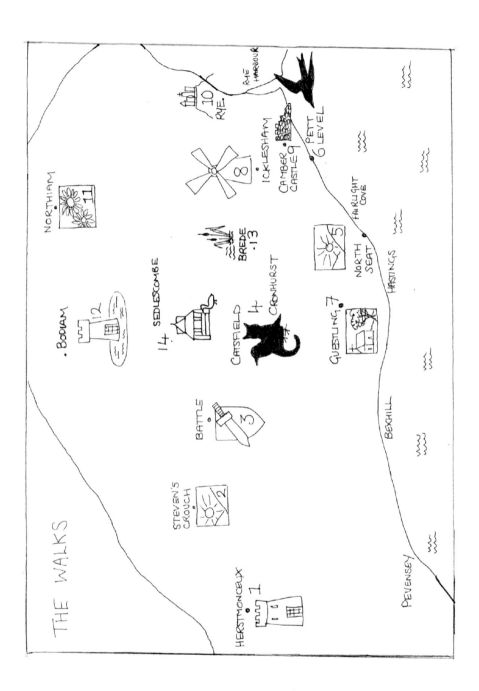

THE WALKS

HERSTMONCEUX · 1

STEVEN'S CROUCH · 2

BATTLE · 3

BODIAM · 12

14. SEDLESCOMBE

CATSFIELD 4 CROWHURST

BREDE · 13

NORTHIAM 11

RYE · 10

RYE HARBOUR

ICKLESHAM

CAMBER CASTLE 9

PETT 6 LEVEL

QUESTLING 7

NORTH SEAT 5

FAIRLIGHT COVE

HASTINGS

BEXHILL

PEVENSEY

- Easy to follow hand-drawn maps by local artist Karin Woolstencroft
- All routes measured using a Garmin Forerunner 405 watch
- Fascinating pieces of local history permeate each route
- Just two maps are needed to cover all the routes – full details provided on each individual walk.
- Full details also provided for parking, refreshments etc
- Useful website details also provided on each walk

3. The Maps

The 1066 routes are covered by just two Ordnance Survey Explorer Maps – 124 Hastings & Bexhill and 125 Romney Marsh, Rye & Winchelsea. However route 12 Bodiam and Sandhurst Cross is easier to follow with the assistance of OS Explorer Map 136 – High Weald.

The relevant map will be shown in the details for each individual walk.

4. Tourist Information Centres & Websites

Within the 1066 area there are three principal Tourist Information Centres based at Battle, Hastings and Rye. Contact details are as follows:

Battle Tourist Information Centre
Battle Abbey, Gatehouse, Battle, East Sussex TN33 OAD
Tele: 01424 776 789
Website: **battletic@rother.gov.uk**

Hastings Tourist Information Centre
Queens Square, Hastings, East Sussex TN34 1TL
Tele: 01424 451 111
Website: **hic@hastings.gov.uk**

Rye Tourist Information Centre
4 -5 Lion Street, Rye, East Sussex TN31 7LB
Tele: 01797 229 049
Website: **ryetic@rother.gov.uk**

Useful website links are given for each individual walk. However two really useful sites for tourist attractions etc are **www.1066country.com** and **www.rother.gov.uk** . Whilst **www.wildhastings.org.uk** is a very informative site on the nature reserves, and the many rare and protected species that live in the 1066 area.

5. Accommodation

Tourists can access the author's website **www.spanglefish.com/1066routes** where there is extensive information on the hotels, guesthouses, camping and caravan sites in the area. Simply click onto the LINKS section on the left hand side. There are also additional photos of each route in the ROUTES – PHOTOS section, in case you need some help in deciding which routes to tackle!

6. The Countryside Code

Please respect the working life of the countryside, as our actions can affect people's livelihoods, our heritage, and the safety and welfare of animals and ourselves.

- Check the weather forecast before you leave, and don't be afraid to turn back if necessary
- Follow the public footpaths wherever possible, particularly when crossing fields where crops are growing. Use gates, stiles or gaps in field boundaries when provided. Climbing over walls, hedges and fences can damage them, and increase the risk of farm animals escaping
- Leave gates as you find them – a farmer will normally leave a gate closed to keep livestock in, but may sometimes leave it open so that they can reach food and water
- Leave machinery and livestock alone, but alert the farmer if you think that an animal is in distress
- Litter and leftover food not only spoils the beauty of the countryside, but can be dangerous to livestock and wildlife, so please take your litter home with you
- Don't damage or remove rocks, plants or trees as they provide home and food for insects, birds and animals
- Dog walkers – by law you must control your dog so that it doesn't scare or disturb farm animals and wildlife. On most areas of open country and common land, known as "access land", you must keep your dog on a short lead between 1st March and 31st July ....and all year round near farm animals. Not only are dogs liable to be shot by a farmer for sheep worrying, but the animals would be shocked and could lose their young. Moreover a dog running amongst cattle is likely to be kicked or even trampled to death. If a farm animal/s chases you and your dog, then it is safer to let the dog off the lead and make for the nearest exit!
- Drive carefully, especially on narrow country lanes

A Farmer's Perspective

Pett farmer Tim Jury is well placed to advise on the countryside, having farmed livestock for many years and also being a keen runner and fellow member of Hastings Runners.

He says: "As with so many enjoyable pursuits walking and running in the countryside comes with a health warning! Seriously though we should remember that we share the countryside with many others, not least the animals providing us with milk, meat, wool, hides and transport etc. Your main concern should be for your own safety and those with you, so when passing through a field with animals such as horses and cattle take care not to scare them by running through their midst. Better to deviate where necessary from the footpath and skirt round a herd or flock; walk or run slowly and steer clear of individual animals that have young, especially cows and their new born calves. It is very rare for animals to attack anyone, unless they are protecting their young.

"Many sheep farmers are becoming increasingly worried by the growing number of sheep worrying incidents. Sheep experience acute distress when worried by unfamiliar dogs, particularly at lambing time, and when new born lambs are separated from their mothers it can then become very difficult to get them to "bond" properly again.

"Most people using a public footpath are potentially an asset to any farmer, as they can see if anything is obviously wrong with livestock or if an animal has fallen into a river. In such an instance do let the farmer know as soon as possible, even if he is just about to sit down to his Sunday lunch! And finally, do please enjoy the beauty of the countryside as it is there to be enjoyed by everyone!"

Herstmonceux Castle.

WALK 1: HERSTMONCEUX

A 4-mile route with stunning views of Herstmonceux Castle, Windmill Hill Mill and surrounding countryside including the South Downs.

- 4.20 miles ascent 773 ft descent 856 ft RATING 2...EASY/MODERATE
- 70% off road paths; 26% quiet lanes; 4% main road (pavement)
- Suitable for walkers and dog walkers; however please note that there are often cows present in some of the fields in sections 2,3 and 4
- OS Explorer Map 124 – Hastings & Bexhill
- Park in the lay-by on Wartling Road, just to the right of the main castle entrance. Wartling Road runs off the A271 from Battle to Herstmonceux
- Start ref: TQ 653103 Postcode: BN27 1RN
- There are no refreshments en route, but on finishing I would highly recommend The Lamb Inn, a delightful 16th century pub in nearby Wartling
- Websites: **www.herstmonceux-castle.com**

Herstmonceux Castle is a magnificent building dating from 1441 with its towers and turrets reflected in the waters of its moats. Set in beautiful parkland and superb Elizabethan gardens, it was built originally as a country house and embodies the history of medieval England and the romance of renaissance Europe. The castle became a ruin and was demolished in 1777, when much of its material was used to build nearby Herstmonceux Place. The castle was restored between 1910 – 1936, and became home to the Royal Greenwich Observatory in 1946. The estate is now owned by the Queen's University of Kingston, Ontario, Canada who opened the Observatory Science Centre in 1995 and have been renovating the domes, buildings and telescopes. The grounds and gardens are open daily during the summer, but the castle isn't open to the public.

Some of the Observatory buildings.

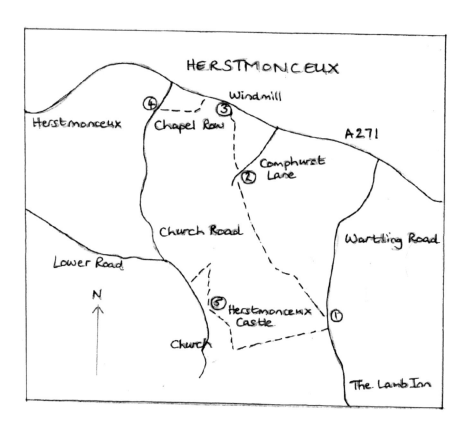

HERSTMONCEUX

Herstmonceux

Windmill

④ --- ③

Chapel Row

A271

② Comphurst Lane

Church Road

Wartling Road

Lower Road

N

⑤ Herstmonceux Castle

①

Church

The Lamb Inn

THE WALK

1. Go through the gate next to the lay-by, and follow the path through the small copse into a field where you will see the **Science Centre** with its extraordinary looking domes ahead of you. Follow the path diagonally across the field to the fence to the right of the Centre, and continue to a stile. Cross over the stile and follow the downhill woodland path, crossing a small footbridge before coming to a junction of paths. Turn left here onto a main track which leads you out of **Plantation Wood** into **The Park,** passing a large pond on your right. Go through the gate at the end of the track, and head uphill across the field to another gate which leads into a much larger field. Continue in the same direction, heading towards a large barn on your left. After passing the barn, go through a gate which brings you out onto an unmade road **Comphurst Lane.**

2. Turn right onto the lane and within 50 yds you will come to a stile on your left. From here you will have a splendid view of **Windmill Hill Mill,** which is the largest post mill in Sussex. Built in 1814 and worked until 1893, it has recently been restored and is now computer controlled with an automatic turning device which relies on wind direction sensors...all clever stuff!
Before you cross the stile however, take a look at the lovely house opposite **Comphurst** which has a superb Norman-style front door. Proceed across the field, which sometimes has horses in, to the next stile; this has quite a drop down into the next field. Now follow a diagonal path downhill and then a short climb to a stile to the right of **Allfree Wood.** Dog walkers should note that there are sometimes cows grazing in this last field. Cross the stile and follow the path round the side of the wood, which emerges on the **A271.**

3. Turn left and continue along the main road which has a wide pavement for 300 yds, before turning into a field driveway with a stile on the left. Cross the stile and follow the track ahead which leads into a very large field. After passing a water trough on the right, go through a gate on the right and follow a straight path with a line of electric fencing on your right. This field also has cows in on occasion. You will pass another water trough within 200 yds; continue to a gate at the edge of the field to the right of a house. Go through this gate and another gate immediately ahead, bringing you out onto **Chapel Row.**

Windmill Hill Mill as seen from Comphurst Lane.

4. The house that you have just passed used to be a pub called variously **The Kicking Donkey** and **The Welcome Stranger...** interestingly Herstmonceux Free Church is literally round the corner! Turn left into Chapel Row, which soon becomes **Church Road,** and enjoy the next mile along this quiet lane which has some delightful cottages and houses. From time to time you will also get some great views of the **South Downs** in the distance to your right. About ¼ mile after passing **Lower Road** on your right, turn left into a gateway making sure that you go through a gate with a bridleway sign. Follow the path across the field with **Herstmonceux Place** over to your left; this impressive looking building was built with bricks from the nearby castle in the late 18th century, and has a fine classical facade. Continue along the path before turning right onto another path which heads up steeply to a gate leading into woodland. There are often cows grazing in this large field.

A splendid view looking back towards Comphurst Lane.

5. Follow the path through the woods for 300 yds until reaching a marker post indicating a junction of paths ahead. Bear left within 20 yds and continue to a stile at the edge of the woods leading you into a field. Head diagonally downhill to a stile, and then cross over the private road to a fenced in path leading to another stile. From here you have a magnificent view of the **castle!** Cross over the stile and follow the path towards the gnarled trunk of an old oak tree ahead; bear left as you approach this and go through the gate ahead. With the castle grounds on your left, follow the path as it heads steadily uphill for over ½ mile until reaching **Wartling Road.** Turn left onto the road, passing the main castle entrance, and the lay-by is right next to this.

14

The view from Steven's Crouch.

WALK 2: STEVEN'S CROUCH

One of the most scenic routes with magnificent views nearly all the way round, in particular the panoramic vista that greets you at the top of Tent Hill. This route of nearly 7 miles also takes in the quaint hamlet of Penhurst with its church and duck pond, and then returns via the Ashburnham forge before a final, steepling climb back up Tent Hill.

- 6.70 miles ascent 1011 ft descent 1028 ft RATING 4 .... TESTING
- 66% off road paths; 9% off road hard track (rural); 23% quiet lanes; 2% main road (grass verge)
- Suitable for walkers and dog walkers; there are invariably sheep in most of the fields in sections 1 and 2, and sometimes cows
- OS Explorer Map 124 Hastings & Bexhill
- Park on the lay-by next to the phone box opposite Crowders Lane on the A271 between Battle and Ashburnham, about ¼ mile after passing

The Squirrel pub on the North Trade Road.
● Start ref: TQ 711153 Postcode: TN33 9LR
● There are no refreshments available en route, but The Squirrel pub is close by and of course Battle itself is only 2 miles away
●   Websites: **www.1066country.com**

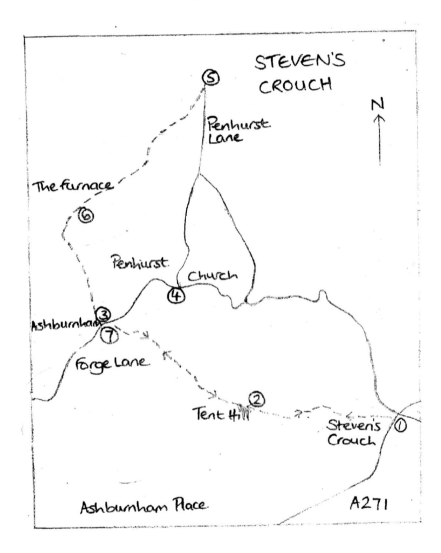

THE WALK

Penhurst may be the lost town of Mercredsburn, which was captured by the Saxon Aella in 491 AD. It is a very old village mentioned in the Domesday Book, but nowadays consists only of the 14th century church, an Elizabethan manor house and a duck pond. **Ashburnham Furnace** was the last iron furnace in Sussex, closed in 1813.

1. Starting at the lay-by on the **A271**, walk past the phone box and the start of **Penhurst Lane** onto a grass verge beside the main road. Continue carefully for 50 yds before turning onto a waymarked path on your right, signposted Ashburnham; you will be following the 1066 Country Walk for the next 2 miles. After crossing a stile just ahead, with **Ashburnham Lodge** on your right, you get your first sight of the superb views which make this such a memorable walk. Head diagonally downhill following the first line of pylons, aiming for a telegraph pole at the right side of a copse. Bear left here, with the copse now on your right, and you will soon see a footpath sign by a water trough at the edge of the copse pointing straight across the next field. Following a line close to the large tree ahead on your left, make your way across to a stile leading into a small wood. The path drops down and then climbs out of the wood into an open field. Bear left and you will see a footpath marker within 100 yds at the edge of a copse. Head straight across the field to the left of the copse opposite; another footpath sign then points you across the field where you are aiming at a stile about 50 yds to the left of a small fir plantation.
You have great views across to your left of **Ashburnham Place**, which was one of the finest country houses in the South East in its heyday. The Ashburnham family controlled the village from the 12th century until 1953 when Lady Catherine, the last in line, died. Much of the house, which had been badly damaged during the Second World War when a fully loaded Marauder bomber crashed nearby, was demolished in 1959. Since being rebuilt it has been used for many years now as a Christian conference centre. The 200 acre park with 3 large lakes was laid out by Capability Brown in the mid 18th century.

2. After crossing the stile aim for a small group of trees ahead and slightly to your right, before plummeting downhill to a stile at the bottom of the field leading into a small wood. Follow the path down a bank to a footbridge, and across another stile which brings you into a narrow field. Go directly across the field to another footbridge over a stream, and cross the stile ahead which

leads into an open field. Proceed straight across the next two fields, which climb very slightly uphill, and are usually full of sheep and on entering the third field bear diagonally right to a gate beside a large garden which used to be a nursery. Follow the path to the end, with a private drive on your right; then bear left across a small paddock going downhill to a stile leading onto **Forge Lane**.

Penhurst Church and duck pond.

3. Turn right onto this quiet lane which soon drops downhill, before a short but steep climb brings you to the hamlet of **Penhurst**. It derives its name from the Anglo-Saxon name "head of the wood", given to this part of the wild forest land of the Weald of Sussex 1000 years ago. The Domesday Book describes it thus: "Penehest, which Osborn holds of the Earl of Eu. The Abbot has half a hide (15 acres), and there are two villeins (common serfs) with two ploughs and one acre of meadow and wood for two hogs. It is worth 15 shillings". Harry H.Corbett of Steptoe & Son fame is buried in the churchyard here.

18

4. Turning left into **Penhurst Lane**, following the signs for Brightling, continue for a mile as the lane climbs steadily uphill. Enjoy the great views across the Beech Estate towards Netherfield on your right. In fact much of the surrounding area comprising nearly 2000 acres forms part of the estate, which boasts some of the largest surviving tracts of ancient meadows typical of the medieval landscape associated with the Weald. Ignore the small lane on your right after ½ mile signposted Battle, and you will soon pass a fine collection of farmhouses in particular **Great Sprays Oast** on your right. Shortly after passing the last farmhouse **Pember Farm**, turn left through a gate into a field.

5. Follow the path as it skirts round the edge of the field, keeping the trees on your right, and then heads downhill. Bear right at the bottom of the field and go through a gap into the next field. Bear left and follow the rutted path around the edge of the field until turning left onto a wide track leading down through woodland to a five bar gate. Go through the gate and follow the bridleway/track downhill until reaching another gate at the bottom. This path can become quite boggy in wet conditions, in which case you can skirt along the edge of the field instead. Go through the gate, with **Rocks Farm** on your right, and follow the track downhill for some way to a footbridge with a ford on your left. This brings you onto a track; over to your right are a group of early cottages, now private residences, which were originally built as one of the ironworks buildings for the **Ashburnham Furnace**. Nearby is evidence of large ponds as the river Ashbourne was dammed with great pools from which water was channelled to power the great drop-hammers to make cannons for the Navy. The furnace was the last of its kind in Sussex, ending in 1813 after a drunken party! The foundry was tended by two furnace men who stoked it with the help of two boys. One of the boys died after drinking a bottle of gin, while the others were so drunk that they forgot to add chalk to the ore. This caused the molten ore to stop flowing, and the furnace became unusable.

6. Continue straight ahead and follow the hard track/unmade road for nearly ¾ mile until it reaches **Forge Lane**. Turn left onto the lane, and within 150 yds you will see a 1066 Country Walk marker post for Steven's Crouch. This is where you originally turned right onto Forge Lane at the end of section 2.

7. Follow your original route for nearly 2 miles back to the start, including the brutal climb up **Tent Hill!**, pictured below.

Battle Abbey.

WALK 3: BATTLE

A 4-mile route starting and finishing outside historic Battle Abbey, with great views of the surrounding countryside.

- 4.20 miles ascent 563 ft descent 552 ft RATING 1 ....EASY
- 49% off road paths; 18% off road hard track (rural); 33% private/unmade road/ quiet lanes
- Suitable for walkers and dog walkers; there are sometimes sheep and cows in section 1, and sheep in a small paddock in section 3
- OS Explorer Map 124 – Hastings & Bexhill

- Parking available either in the Mount Street car park, just behind Battle High Street, or in the car park in Park Lane, 100 yds past the Abbey.
- Battle rail station, on the London - Hastings line. 5 minutes walk from the start.
- Start ref: TQ 749157 Postcode: TN33 OAD
- Refreshments – you are spoilt for choice in Battle, but being a cake connoisseur I would plump for the carrot cake at A Taste of Battle tea rooms where you can sit outside with a splendid view of the Abbey!
- Websites: **www.1066country.com**

Battle Abbey is famous worldwide and was founded to commemorate the 1066 Battle of Hastings nearby. The original gatehouse is still intact, as are some parts of the Abbey despite the dissolution of the monasteries in Henry VIII's reign. You can walk round the original battlefield and actually stand on the spot where King Harold was slain. The town of **Battle** was gradually built around the Abbey, and later was a main producer of gunpowder. Most of the area was heavily wooded, and provided oak and other timbers for Navy shipyards, cannonballs and gunpowder.

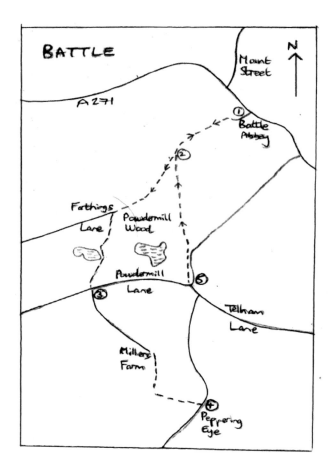

THE WALK

1. Starting outside the Abbey, continue along **Park Lane** past the car park onto a hard track which leads to a gate opening into **George Meadow & Upper Stumblets.** This is pretty well the halfway point of the Pevensey to Rye 1066 Country Walk. Go through the gate and continue along a track with woodland on your left for 600 yds, until reaching a marker post at the top of the hill which gives you wonderful countryside views. Bear right here following the Pevensey signs, and you can enjoy a lovely downhill section to a gate in the bottom right hand corner of this field. Please note that there are sometimes cows grazing both along the track and in this field.

The view towards Powdermill Wood.

2. Go through the gate and follow the woodland path to the next gate. You may be lucky enough to spot some free range organic pigs rooting about in the woods to your left! Go through the gate and within 50 yds cross over the stile on your left; there is a house on your right. Cross the field to a stile leading into **Powdermill Wood.** Follow the narrow path as it wends its way downhill, bearing right all the time and ignoring paths to your left. The path brings you down to **Farthing Pond,** where you continue with the large pond on your right to a small footbridge over a stream. Follow the hard track which rises steeply uphill onto a softer path, and continue to a gate at the end of the path which brings you out onto **Powdermill Lane.** In 1676 John Hammond was licensed to build a powdermill on land owned by Battle Abbey. Other mills then sprang up in the area, and were said to make the finest gunpowder in Europe supplying the British Army right up to the Crimean War. The works were closed in 1874 after a series of disastrous explosions. Nearby **Powder Mills Hotel** is built on the site of the gunpowder works.

The author meets a "handsome" Saddleback pig close to the
woodland path in the first part of section 2!

3. Take care crossing over Powdermill Lane, which can be quite busy, and
proceed down the private road to **Millers Farm** for nearly ¾ mile. Passing
North and **South Cottages** early on, you have great views towards **Telham.** It
was from Telham Hill where William The Conqueror's army advanced towards
the English army forming up on Senlac Hill. Follow the road past **Millers Oast,**
but as it starts to bear right towards some farm buildings go over a stile next to
a gate immediately ahead. Continue to the next stile, where there is a junction
of footpath signs....bear right and head across to the next stile which has a large
circular building on your right. Go over the stile into a small paddock, which
usually has sheep in, and this quickly leads onto a track which drops downhill
between fenced in fields to a large metal gate. However here you bear left over a
stile/gate, and continue along the edge of the field until reaching a stile beside
Stumblet's Wood. Follow the narrow path with the wood on your immediate
left, which widens out onto a track which soon emerges on **Peppering Eye,**
another private road.

4. Turn left onto the road by **Powdermill Cottage,** and follow it for nearly a mile to its junction with **Telham Lane.** You will pass **Peppering Eye Farm** and **Old Peppering Eye Farmhouse,** before reaching a gate at the end of the road where you turn left into Telham Lane. Within 100 yds you reach the busy junction with **Powdermill Lane;** take great care as you cross over the road to a steep bank with a stile at the top.

5. Follow the path gradually uphill, running parallel to the lane; **Powdermill House** is over to your left. Go over the stile at the top, and cross the private road to the stile opposite. This leads onto a hard track which drops downhill, with a fenced in field on your left, until reaching a softer track heading uphill through two gates. You then have a steep climb aiming for the solitary tree at the top of the hill, but it keeps on climbing for another 100 yds until levelling off just before the marker post that you passed in section 1. Bear right after the post, and follow your original path back to the **Abbey.**

A steepling climb to rejoin the track leading back to the Abbey!

The manor house ruins in Crowhurst.

WALK 4: CROWHURST

One of my favourite longer routes at 8.50 miles; extremely scenic with some superb views going out along Powdermill Stream, then from Henley's Down towards Watermill and on the final leg looking back down into the valley towards Crowhurst. You pass close to Fore Wood, an RSPB nature reserve, and the historic village of Catsfield.

- 8.50 miles ascent 859 ft descent 817 ft RATING 4 .... TESTING
- 57% off road paths; 13% off road hard track (rural); 30% quiet lanes
- Suitable for walkers and dog walkers; there are invariably sheep grazing in some of the fields in sections 1,3,7 and 10 and sometimes cows in the first two fields at the start and finish of the route
- OS Explorer Map 124 Hastings & Bexhill
- Park at the bottom of Station Road which is opposite St. George Church, Forewood Lane, Crowhurst

- Crowhurst rail station, on the London - Hastings line, is 5 minutes walk from the start.
- Start ref: TQ 757122 Postcode: TN33 9AJ
- Refreshments are available at The White Hart Inn, Catsfield at the 5.50 mile mark, or at The Plough, Crowhurst, 2 mins drive from the finish
- Websites: **www.rspb.org.uk/reserves/guide/f/forewood**

The earliest mention of Crowhurst was in 771 when King Offa of Mercia gave the Bishop of Selsey a piece of land there, known as "Croghyrst". In return the bishop built a church there for the population. Before 1066 the manor was owned by King Harold, and was completely destroyed by the Normans before the Battle of Hastings.

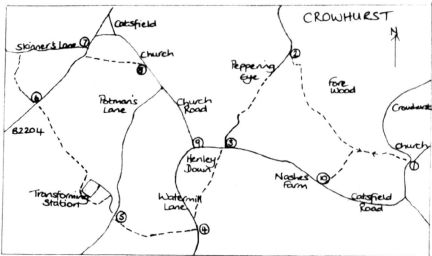

THE WALK

1. Cross over **Forewood Lane** into the private drive opposite for **Court Lodge.** You soon see the ruins of an old manor house built by Walter de Scotney, one of the knights who accompanied Richard I on his 3rd crusade in the 12th century. He was executed in 1259 after being accused of trying to murder his employer the Earl of Gloucester. You may want to have a quick look round **St. George Church** first as the churchyard boasts the oldest yew tree in Britain, over 40 feet in circumference and possibly circa 3000 years old! Go through the gate at the end of the drive, and follow the path across the field to the gate opposite, which leads into a much larger field. Enjoy the views as you head across the field down towards **Powdermill Stream.** Ignoring the footbridge close to the oak tree, continue alongside the stream going over three footbridges which link each field. After crossing the last footbridge, turn right and continue now with the stream and Fore Wood immediately on your right until reaching the entrance to **Fore Wood.** The RSPB nature reserve is one of the largest tracts of ancient woodland remaining in the South East. It has been used as a coppiced woodland for at least 500 years, and Roman bell pits are found throughout the reserve. The woodland supports many birds and wildlife including woodpeckers, migrant warblers etc. At the entrance to the wood, turn left and follow the track uphill across the centre of the field to a footpath marker post. Turn right through a gate onto a track leading uphill to **Peppering Eye**, emerging opposite **Powdermill Cottage.**

2. Turn left here and continue along a track which climbs slowly uphill for ¼ mile, going past two pretty cottages **(Forewood Cottages)** until reaching a gate at the end of the track. Go through the gate and the clearing across to your left, and then bear right heading downhill across the field to the bottom where you reach a junction of footpaths and bridleways. Follow the bridleway which goes uphill, and then swings round to the right past a pond and then **Catsfield Place Farm** before going uphill again. Bear right at the top, with the entrance to **Catsfield Place** on your left. In 1791 Princess Lamballe, one of Marie Antoinette's ladies in waiting, was sent with the queen's jewels for safe keeping to Lady Gibbs at Catsfield Place. Bearing right, follow the track as it leads out to the main road, **Crowhurst Road.**

3. Cross over the road onto the farm track opposite. After 100 yds bear right and follow the path along the edge of the field until dropping down over a gate on your left into the next field. From here you have some stunning views from

The view from Henley's Down towards Watermill.

Henley's Down towards Watermill. Follow the path downhill keeping the line of trees immediately on your left, and go through a gap into the next field. The path continues downhill skirting to the right of **Tilden's Wood,** until reaching a stile at the bottom. Cross this and follow the woodland path beside a small stream which emerges on **Watermill Lane.**

4. Turn left onto **Watermill Lane,** and after 100 yds turn right into the driveway for **The Old Watermill.** The public footpath runs beside the right of the house, and leads into a field at the back. Follow a well trodden path across three fields which lead one into another, and then go over a stile beside **Watermill Stream** into the next field. Follow the path across the field to a gate leading onto **Potman's Lane.**

5. Cross the lane into the entrance for **Ninfield Sub-Station.** Turn left through a gate immediately after the cattle grid, and follow the path ahead which soon swings round to the right. This then drops down to a track beside **Watermill Stream,** and continue with the sub-station on your right to a gate. Go through the gate and after 50 yds bear right beside a pylon; cross the stile ahead into the next field. Follow the path a short distance to another stile which leads into **Reed Wood** on your left. Follow the centre track through the wood, before bearing left as another track merges from the right and go a short distance to a gate at the end of the track. Head straight across the next two fields until reaching a gate which leads onto a private drive. Follow this drive for 200 yds until reaching the main **B2204** road at **Catsfield Bridge.**

6. Take great care crossing this busy main road to the track opposite, which leads up past a delightful farmhouse, **Hophouse Farm.** At the end of the track turn right through a gate, then bear left and skirt round the edge of the field until reaching a stile on your left as you start going downhill. Cross the stile and footbridge, then bear right and head downhill to a stile. Cross the stile and head uphill across a field, where horses are always grazing, leading up past a stable block onto **Skinners Lane.** Turn right and continue along the lane for nearly ½ mile until reaching the **B2204** once again. For those of you who want refreshments, with just over 3 miles to go!, turn left here and **The White Hart, Catsfield** is close by. After refuelling cross into **Church Road** and continue along until reaching **St. Laurence Church** at the start of section 8.

7. Those not needing refreshments can turn right onto the **B2204,** and continue for 100 yds along the pavement until reaching **Highrise Cottage.** Take extreme care crossing the main road to the bank opposite, and cross the stile into a field from where you have a great view of the two churches in the village of Catsfield. Continue across the field to a stile, and then follow a path between farm buildings until reaching a stile at the end of the path. The path then goes diagonally across a field towards **St. Laurence Church** on **Church Road.**

8. Cross the road and go up through the churchyard of this 13th century church which is shaded by one of the oldest oak trees in East Sussex. The famous railway engineer Thomas Brassey is buried here. He built Britain's Great Northern Railway, Canada's Great Trunk railway, as well as railways across the Alps, Argentina, India and Australia! Exiting the churchyard continue along the path at the top of the bank for a short distance before rejoining **Church Road.** Continue along the lane for ½ mile until reaching **Henley's Down.**

9. At Henley's Down bear left, and continue uphill following the signs for Crowhurst; you are now on **Crowhurst Road.** As the climb levels off you will pass by the track to Catsfield Place which you came up in section 2. Continue along the lane for a further ¾ mile, and take in the glorious views down into the valley on your left until reaching the **Crowhurst** road sign.

10. Go over the stile on your left just beyond the road sign, and enjoy the ¾ mile back to the start which is one of my favourite stretches in this book! You have a fantastic view towards **Crowhurst** as you follow the path down into the valley. You pass a pond on your left, and then entering the next field keep the line of trees on your right before dropping sharply downhill to a gate, quickly followed by a footbridge over **Powdermill Stream** which you passed in section 1. Turn right here and retrace your steps back to the start.

The splendid view down towards Crowhurst.

| The view from North's Seat. |

WALK 5: NORTH'S SEAT

One of the most scenic routes with some spectacular views across to the coast, but also probably the most testing route! North's Seat, on the edge of Hastings Country Park, is the highest point in Hastings and on a clear day you can see the coast of France with the naked eye! The route goes down through the valley into Pett, and then a mid-section loop around the village, before a tough climb back to the start. En route you also pass Fairlight Hall, an impressive Victorian gothic mansion, and have fine views for most of the way of the surrounding countryside.

- 6.80 miles ascent 992 ft descent 964 ft RATING 5 .... VERY TESTING!
- 69% off road paths; 7% off road hard track (rural); 24% private/unmade roads/quiet lanes
- Suitable for walkers and dog walkers; there are often sheep and sometimes cows in two fields at the end of section 3, and also sheep in

several fields in sections 5,6 and 8
- OS Explorer Map 124 Hastings & Bexhill
- Park near the junction of Martineau Lane and Mill Lane, just off the A259 Hastings to Rye Road, ½ mile beyond Ore going towards Guestling
- Start ref: TQ 842123 Postcode: TN35 5DR
- Refreshments are available at The Two Sawyers pub in Pett, a friendly traditional hostelry a third of the way into the route
- Websites: **www.wildhastings.org.uk/reserves/hcp.aspx**

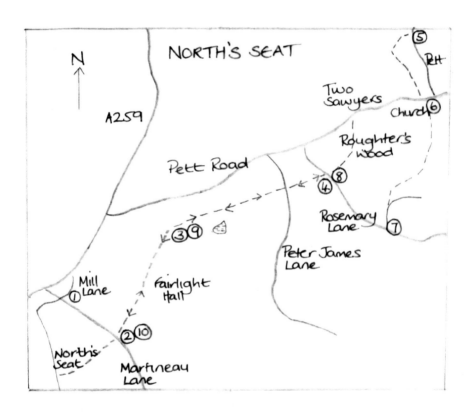

THE WALK

1. Cross over **Martineau Lane** into the continuation of **Mill Lane,** a hard track which climbs steeply up to North's Seat. Bear left as the track swings round after 200 yds, and in another 200 yds you pass a telecoms mast on your left. **North's Seat** itself is another 300 yds further along on your right. There was once a windmill on this spot, which is 575 ft above sea level. Later a lookout platform was erected by Frederick North, former mayor of Hastings and local MP, which no longer exists. The views from here are incredible ....on a clear day you can see for more than 60 miles across the Downs and Weald to the west, as well as the French coast!

My partner Helen surveying the Channel!

Continue for another 100 yds before turning left by a footpath signpost for Fairlight Road. After another 100 yds cross over a track straight ahead, and follow the 1066 Hastings walk signs as the enclosed path between fields drops downhill to **Martineau Lane.**

2. Cross over the lane to a stile opposite, still following the 1066 signs. Follow the path on the right hand side of the field, before turning left across the centre of the field. You have a fine view of **Fairlight Hall** from here – an impressive Victorian gothic mansion, imitation Tudor, built at the turn of the 20th century. Turn right at the footpath sign, and continue downhill with a hedgerow on your left until turning left through a gap in the hedgerow leading into another field. Bear right here across the field, keeping a pylon on your right hand side, until going through a narrow entrance into woodland. Follow the path downhill until crossing two footbridges; then climb up a steep bank before going diagonally across a small field to a gap beside a gate.

3. Cross over a private drive to the stile opposite, and proceed straight across the next three fields, going over a stile in each instance. The final stile leads you into a small wood. Cross over another stile to exit the wood, and follow the path downhill across the centre of the field. You get a great view from here of Pett church in the distance. At this point you will be leaving the 1066 Hastings walk. Cross over two stiles in quick succession to drop down into the next field, and follow the path to a stile near the bottom left hand corner. Cross over **Peter James Lane** and a private drive to the stile opposite, and follow the path across the next two fields to a stile emerging on **Rosemary Lane.** @@

4. Cross over the lane to a stile opposite, and follow a narrow path with horse paddocks on your left. At the end of the path cross a stile into **Roughter's Wood,** and follow the path as it climbs gently at first before a steep final 200 yds up onto **Pett Road.** Turn right and **The Two Sawyers pub** is opposite you. Continue along Pett Road for 600 yds (there is a pavement on the right hand side) before turning left opposite **St. Mary & St. Peter Church,** which is an interesting church built in the 1860s. It has a tall octagonal belfry, with large gargoyles staring down from it. Follow the enclosed path between houses to a stile at the bottom, and then head downhill across two fields aiming for the bottom left hand corner next to a pond. Here you arrive at a junction of tracks by a gate. Cross over the stile on your right, following the Nature Reserve signs. This enclosed path soon leads you into a short section of woodland, whose path emerges on **Pannel Lane.** You have now reached the halfway point of the route.

5. Turn right onto Pannel Lane, and continue uphill for 500 yds until reaching the junction with **Pett Road.** Turn right and quickly cross over the road to go through a gate beside the church.

6. Follow the path to a stile in the left hand corner, and then continue directly ahead across a field to the next stile. Cross over this and pause to admire the excellent views across to **Fairlight,** in particular **Fairlight Church** which can be seen for miles around – built in 1843 its turreted towers stand 562 ft above sea level. Continue downhill with a horse paddock on your right. Go over a stile into the next field, still going downhill, and bear left beside a pond until you reach another stile. There is a large rock in front of this, and a stile a short distance ahead. Follow the path as it continues downhill with a hedgerow on your right. Bear right at the bottom of the field, and go down a bank and across a narrow field to a footbridge. After crossing the bridge you face a sharp uphill climb to a stile at the top of this field! Ignore the footpath signs on your left about halfway up. Cross the stile into the next field, and head across the field for 150 yds until going over a stile beside a gate leading to a private drive to **Low Winters Farm.** Turn right and follow this for 200 yds until reaching **Rosemary Lane.**

Views across to Fairlight.

7. Turn right and continue along Rosemary Lane for 650 yds, passing some pretty, thatched cottages in particular **Stream Cottage** on your right. Just after passing **Lower New Barn Farm** on your right, cross over the stile on your left beside a gate. This is where you crossed the lane at the end of section 3. *@@*

8. and 9. Follow the reverse route in sections 2 and 3, which is now mainly uphill, all the way back to **Martineau Lane.**

10. However upon reaching Martineau Lane, this time turn right and continue for 600 yds back to the start.

The Royal Military Canal at Pett Level.

WALK 6: PETT LEVEL

A delightful route of just over 6 miles starting out along the Royal Military Canal and then through Pannel Valley Nature Reserve. Returning via Pett Village which has some lovely views across to Fairlight, and then a superb cliff top path finish down to Cliff End.

- 6.25 miles ascent 639ft descent 620 ft RATING 3 .... MODERATE
- 75% off road paths; 10% off road hard track (rural); 15% private/unmade roads/quiet lanes
- Suitable for walkers and dog walkers; there are invariably sheep and sometimes cows grazing by the canal in section 1, and sometimes sheep in sections 3 and 4
- OS Explorer Map 124 Hastings & Bexhill
- Park in the Smuggler Inn car park on Pett Level Road. From Hastings, turn right at Ore onto Fairlight Road which descends down Battery Hill to

Pett Level
- Start ref: TQ 890134 Postcode: TN35 4EH
- Refreshments are available at the Smuggler Inn opposite, or at the Royal Oak in Pett Village which is just over halfway round the route
- Websites: **www.winchelsea.net/visiting/welcome.htm**

Pett was first mentioned in the Domesday Book and was known then as "Luet". Pett Level is a wide expanse of land which is a haven for wildfowl. The Royal Military Canal which runs from Cliff End at Pett Level to Seabrook, nr Hythe, was barely finished before it was realised what a pointless exercise this 28 mile project was. The Napoleonic Army, having conquered Europe's greatest rivers, was hardly likely to be defeated by a 30 ft wide canal if and when they crossed the English Channel!

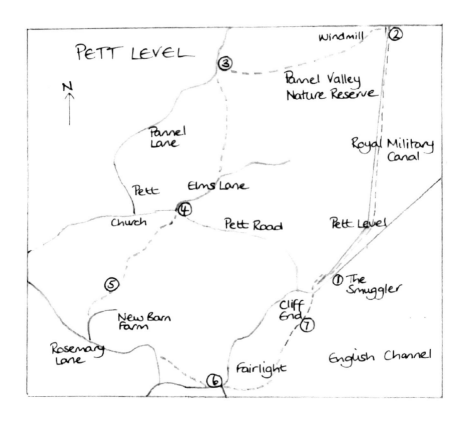

THE WALK

1. Starting in the Smuggler Inn car park, turn right onto the path beside the **Royal Military Canal** which forms part of the Saxon Shore Way. This runs from Hastings to Gravesend in Kent, basically following the South East coastline as it was 1500 years ago. Continue for 1.50 miles with the canal on your left hand side, until reaching a footbridge on your left which crosses over the canal.

2. Proceed to the footbridge immediately ahead which takes you into the **Pannel Valley nature reserve**. This is detailed extensively in Icklesham and Pannel Valley Route 8. Continue for ¾ mile with a stream on your right, passing through two gates and ignoring all other turnings and footbridges. This section has a short section of hard track and an even shorter stretch of unmade road. You can see Sir Paul McCartney's windmill high up on your right, and farmland across to your left. At the end of the path cross over a stile at **Pannel Bridge** and turn left onto **Pannel Lane.**

3. After passing the cattle grid entrance to **Pannel Farm** on your left, go over the stile almost immediately on your left and cross the field to the stile opposite which is just to the right of the farm. You then face quite a testing little climb to the next stile. Go over this stile and cross the field, dropping down towards a small wood where a footbridge leads you into the next field. Follow the path on the left hand side of the field, before going over a stile/gate onto **Elms Lane.** Turn right and continue for 600 yds slightly uphill along the lane into **Pett,** where you will find **The Royal Oak** on your left. This is your only chance for refreshments before you reach the end of the route!

4. Cross over **Pett Road** to a gate which leads you into **Pett Recreation Ground.** Follow the path across to a stile which takes you into a field with superb views of the surrounding countryside. Head diagonally across to a stile/gate on your left, and follow the path as it winds its way downhill towards a copse with a pond which will be on your right. Here you join another path and bear left, crossing a stile down into the next field. Follow this downhill to the stile at the bottom, and continue down for a short distance to a footbridge.

5. After crossing the footbridge, you face a wicked climb uphill to the next stile!

41

After catching your breath, proceed across the field to the stile immediately ahead which brings you out onto the track leading to **Low Winters Farm,** which is across to your left. Turn right and follow the track onto **Rosemary Lane.** Turn left and continue along the lane for nearly ½ mile ignoring the first two footpath markers on your left. However as you go round a right hand bend cross over the stile on your left, and proceed straight across the field slightly uphill to a stile. This brings you out onto the driveway to **Wakehams Farm.** Turn right and within 50 yds cross over the stile on your left and head directly across two paddocks which usually have horses in. The last stile brings you into a scrubby field. Follow the path as it heads downhill but watch out for the large number of very deep rabbit holes on this path! Go down a bank at the bottom, and you will see a gate on your right which leads out onto **Pett Level Road.**

6. Turn left and within 100 yds cross over into **Stream Lane,** and go through the gate immediately on your left. This is marked **National Trust – Fairlight Cliffs.** Scramble diagonally up the extremely steep hillside!, until entering the next field where it mercifully levels off. Bear right, keeping a fence on your right, following the path to a stile which leads you onto the cliff top path. Take time to enjoy the splendid view across to **Fairlight Cove** (below).

Turn left onto the path and continue all the way along the cliff top, watching out for the many tree stumps and roots lying in wait! **Dogs should be on a lead as the vegetation on your right is only yards away from the edge of the cliff!**

7. At the end of the field the path narrows, as it winds its way downhill past an interesting array of houses and gardens on your left. You have some dramatic views on your right out to sea. Turn right at the bottom of the path onto **Pett Level Road,** and continue for 300 yds until turning left onto an unmade road **Canal Bank** which is opposite Pett Level car park. This marks the start of the **Royal Military Canal** at Cliff End. Continue for another 300 yds before crossing a footbridge on your right over the canal, leading directly back to the car park.

Guestling Church.

WALK 7: GUESTLING

An extremely picturesque route of 7 miles with some superb views of Guestling, the Brede Valley, Doleham and Westfield. I have to confess that this is my favourite route ... the panoramic view from the track leading down to Lower Snaylham in section 3 is worth doing this route for alone! Much of the route Includes parts of the 1066 Country Walk and the 1066 Hastings Walk.

- 7.00 miles ascent 708 ft descent 636 ft RATING 3 .... MODERATE
- 67% off road paths; 10% off road hard track (rural); 17% private/unmade roads/quiet lanes; 6% main road (half on pavements)
- Suitable for walkers and dog walkers; there are usually sheep grazing in some of the fields in sections 2 and 6, and occasionally cows in one field just before Great Maxfield in section 6
- OS Explorer Map 124, Hastings & Bexhill
- Parking available in the car park at St. Laurence Church. Coming out of

Hastings on the A259 to Rye, turn right after passing Guestling Primary School into Church Lane and the church is 400 yds along the lane
- Start ref: TQ 855144 Postcode: TN35 4LS
- Refreshments are available at The Three Oaks pub, 1.25 miles from the finish
- Websites: **www.1066country.com**

Guestling is one of 3 villages mentioned in the Domesday Book as being part of the rape of Gestlinges. **St. Laurence Church** where the route starts from was founded in Anglo-Saxon times, its towers built after the Norman conquest. Olive Brockwell, immortalised as Alice by A.E. Milne (changing guards at Buckingham Palace, Christopher Robin went down with Alice) is buried in the churchyard, the inscription paid for by Christopher Milne (the original Christopher Robin).

@/@ Alternative route for dog walkers.

THE WALK

1. Go through the gate in the car park into the churchyard, and follow the path to the gate at the opposite side near the church. Cross over to the path opposite, which leads downhill between hedgerows to a metal gate with a pond on your left. Go through the gate and follow the path across the centre of a large crop field, which drops down to a gateway into the next field with a pond on your right. Bear left and follow the path along the bottom of this field, which then swings round to the right with a steady uphill climb, keeping a hedgerow on your left. Before reaching the top of the hill, go through a gap in the hedgerow on your left next to what remains of an old stile, and follow the path uphill across the centre of the next field until reaching the stile at the top. This brings you out onto the busy **A259** road.

2. @@ I have an alternative route, in particular for dog walkers, wishing to avoid the next 500 yds section along the A259 – please see @@ at the end of this route. Otherwise turn right and take great care crossing over this busy main road. Continue for 500 yds passing a lay-by on your right before going over a stile on your left opposite **Oak Pond Kennels.** Follow the path downhill through an apple orchard, turning right at the bottom and crossing over a stile in the far corner. Head downhill across the centre of the field, before bearing right as the woodland on your right peters out, and then cross a small ditch. Go up a small bank, and continue ahead to a gate beside a small and very picturesque lake on your right. Turn right, keeping the lake on your right, and follow the path gradually uphill to a stile next to a small cottage which brings you out onto a quiet lane **Broad Street.**

3. Turn left and continue along the lane for 200 yds, before turning left over a cattle grid after passing two cottages. You will see signs for the 1066 Country Walk, which you will now be following for the next 2.5 miles. Follow the hard track as it passes **Snaylham House** on your left and then **The Old Farmhouse** on your right. @@ **Those taking the alternative route will rejoin us shortly after this.** Follow the track as it climbs slightly uphill to a metal gate, and then drops down towards **Lower Snaylham.** The view from this ridge over towards Guestling on your left, Doleham straight ahead and the Brede Valley on your right is one of my favourites in the 1066 area.

Views from the track leading towards Lower Snaylham.

4. After passing a barn on your right, cross over a stile at the end of the track next to a gate. With a farmhouse on your right, go over the stile opposite which leads downhill to another stile. Turn right into a long, narrow field and halfway along bear left by a footpath marker over an earth bridge between fields. Follow the path around the edge of this next field for most of the way round, until bearing right to follow a path across two footbridges in quick succession. As you enter the next field, where there are sometimes horses in, bear left across the field to another footbridge. Head diagonally across this field, also often containing horses, to a metal gate at the top. Follow the path uphill, which takes you past **Lower Lidham Hill Farm** onto **Lidham Hill.**

5. Turn right onto **North Lane,** which sweeps uphill before levelling off to give you some great views over the Brede Valley and Westfield. Continue past **Doleham Lane** on your right, and then as the lane bears round to the left go through the gate on your right. Turn right after the pond, and follow the path downhill into a wooded section where you should take great care crossing the Ore – Ashford **railway line.** After crossing a stile into a field, head downhill to a footbridge over **Doleham Ditch,** a tributary of the River Brede.

Crossing the Doleham Ditch.

6. After crossing the footbridge turn left, at which point you will be leaving the 1066 Country Walk and instead joining the 1066 Hastings Walk for the remainder of the route. Follow the path alongside the stream until crossing a footbridge on your left, then follow an enclosed path between fields across a couple of stiles until going over another stile into a much larger field. Follow the path across the field leading to a stile in the top right hand corner, with a barn across to your left. This brings you onto a track facing **Great Maxfield,** a very pretty hamlet. Turn left and follow the track uphill for 200 yds to a stile. As you cross the stile you can enjoy some more splendid views of Westfield, which is the village where I live! Turn immediately left over another stile onto a path over the railway bridge. Cross the next stile and follow the path across a field to a stile. Now follow the path across the centre of the next three fields, then bearing right as you enter the next field and following the path to a gate which brings you out onto a private road close to **The Three Oaks pub;** this is your chance to stop for refreshments!

7. Turn left after going through the gate, and then left again by the pub onto **Butcher's Lane.** Continue along the lane for 500 yds, before going through a gate on your right signposted 1066 Hastings Walk, next to a track to **Half House Farm.** The path leads diagonally across the field to a stile in the top left hand corner, and then heads across two more fields before going through a gate onto a woodland path. Turn right at the end of the path onto the **A259,** and continue for 250 yds along the pavement until reaching the turning for **Church Lane** on your left. Take care crossing this busy road into the lane. Within 100 yds follow the footpath signs on your left, and continue along a bank running parallel to the lane until reaching the church.

@@ **For those using the alternative route at the start of section 2,** turn left onto the grass verge of the **A 259** and continue along for 100 yds until crossing over into the track leading down to **Harborough Nurseries.** Bear left beside the nursery car park, and follow a track which sweeps round behind the car park down to a gate. Go through the gate, with a barn on your left, and follow a path across the centre of the field to a stile. Cross this and follow the path ahead across a much smaller field which leads into woodland. Continue along the path, ignoring all turnings, which eventually slopes downhill to a small stream which you will need to jump across! Go up the bank on the other side, and then bear left following the path uphill across a very scrubby field. About 2/3rds the way uphill, go through an entrance by a footpath marker into the next field which is on your left. Turn right and head up to a wide track opposite a pond. Turn left onto the track, and you will have rejoined the main route at @@ in section 3. This short cut will take ¾ mile off your route.

A superb panoramic view awaits from the windmill!

WALK 8: ICKLESHAM

A very peaceful, scenic route of nearly 4 miles with superb views most of the way round including the well known local windmill above, owned by Sir Paul McCartney, which looks out over the Brede Valley and across to Pett Level. The route also takes in the Royal Military Canal and Pannel Valley Nature Reserve.

- 3.90 miles ascent 650 ft descent 634 ft RATING 1 .... EASY
- 77% off road paths; 10% off road hard track (rural); 13% quiet lanes
- Suitable for walkers and dog walkers; however there are usually sheep and cows grazing on Hog Hill (section 3) and alongside the Royal Military Canal stretch (section 4)
- OS Explorer Map 124 Hastings & Bexhill
- Park close to the junction of Laurel Lane and Workhouse Lane, Icklesham, where there is space on a wide grass lay-by. Both lanes run off the main A259 road between Hastings and Rye

- Start ref: TQ 879162 Postcode: TN36 4AJ
- Refreshments are available close by at The Queens Head Inn in Parsonage Lane, Icklesham. Built in 1632 this historic pub has wonderful views over the Brede valley towards Udimore and Winchelsea, and won the 2009 CAMRA award for real ale in South East Sussex.
- Websites: www.winchelsea.net/visiting/welcome.htm

Icklesham probably derived its name from the Anglo-Saxon "Iclingas Ham", the home of the Iclas family. The first record was in 772 when it appeared as "Icoleshamme" in a land charter signed by King Offa of Mercia. In early days it dominated the River Brede, and would have been a prime target for the Normans when they landed in 1066.

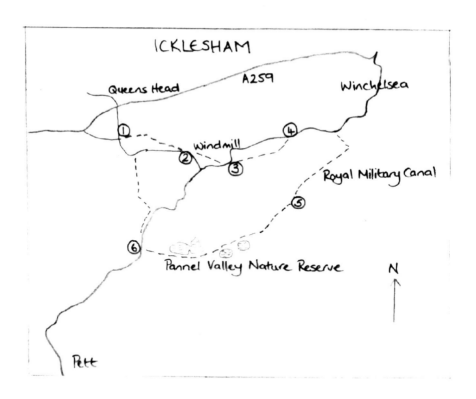

THE WALK

1. Starting at the junction of **Laurel Lane** and **Workhouse Lane,** go into the driveway immediately opposite which is to the left of two cottages. You will see a gate 50 yds ahead with a stile on the right hand side. Go over the stile and follow the path as it winds its way through a large apple orchard, ignoring a stile on your right hand side. Soon you will come to a large metal gate which opens onto the private driveway to **Manor Farm;** you can see the fine oast house across to your left. Cross to a small gate opposite and continue following the footpath signs through the orchards bearing slightly to the right, you will get glimpses from time to time of the windmill up ahead. You will then pass through a gateway in the hedge on your right hand side onto **Windmill Lane.** Signs denote that this part of the route is on the 1066 Country Walk.

2. Turn left onto **Windmill Lane** and within 50 yds on your left hand side is another stile with a splendid view up to the windmill. Take time when you have reached the top of the hill to admire the magnificent panoramic views with Brede Valley on your left, Winchelsea straight ahead and Pett Level across to your right. The old post **windmill** which has been restored has found a new use in the last 30 years, having been bought as a recording studio by Sir Paul McCartney. At the bottom of the hill cross over a stile onto **Wickham Rock Lane.** Turn left and continue for 150 yds.

3. As the lane bears round to the left, cross over a stile immediately ahead next to a gate. Continue across the field, and cross over two stiles into the next field. Continue straight ahead and enjoy the excellent views across to Pett Level on your right. As you pass through a gateway into the next field, the path bears round to the left and starts going downhill to a gate where you rejoin **Wickham Rock Lane.** Dog walkers note that there are invariably sheep grazing in these last two fields and sometimes cows as well!

4. Turn right onto the lane, and continue downhill for ¼ mile. As the lane starts to sweep round to the left, cross over the stile on your right hand side. Follow the path downhill heading towards a footbridge over the **Royal Military Canal;** after going through a gateway turn right just before the footbridge. Continue alongside the canal for nearly ½ mile with a bank on your right hand side. The canal was excavated in 1804 when the threat of Napoleon's invasion was at its height. The canal runs 28 miles from Cliff End (you can see this about 1.50

miles ahead of you, nestling at the foot of Fairlight!) and Seabrook, nr. Hythe in Kent ....a monumental project of its time! Dog walkers, again be aware that this stretch of the canal usually contains both sheep and cows.

5. After ½ mile a stream runs into the canal from your right hand side, with the delightful name of the **Pannel Sewer!**, and you will see a small footbridge over this about 30 yds to your right. Cross this bridge, and then another smaller footbridge almost immediately on your right. This leads you into the **Pannel Valley Nature Reserve,** which consists of circa 400 acres of farmland which has been converted in recent years to a series of reed beds, lakes, scrubland and woodland areas. This provides a haven to all types of birds including red kites and marsh harriers, as well as ducks, geese etc. Continue for ¾ mile with the stream on your right hand side, passing through two gates and ignoring all other turnings and footbridges. This section has a short section of hard track and an even shorter section of unmade road. You will see the windmill high up to your right, and farmland across to your left. At the end of the path cross over a stile at **Pannel Bridge,** and turn right onto **Pannel Lane.**

Pannel Bridge.

6. Continue a short distance along **Pannel Lane,** which then becomes **Pett Lane,** and immediately after passing the entrance to **Little Pannel Farm** on your left climb up a stepped bank also on the left. Follow the path round to the right as it climbs uphill, running parallel to the lane with a copse on your left. You will soon reach a point where the path divides just before an old wall. Bear left here and follow the path as it winds its way initially downhill with a large pond on your right, before swinging round to the right to join a larger track. Bear right as the tracks merge and head uphill with trees on either side. Upon reaching a fenced in field in front of you, cross over the stile which is slightly to your left and head straight across the field to the next gate/stile. Continue ahead with an apple orchard now on your right, and then the last gate/stile brings you out onto **Windmill Lane.** Turn left and the finish is just 300 yds along the lane.

Camber Castle.

WALK 9: CAMBER CASTLE

A very enjoyable route of nearly 6 miles, featuring Camber Castle and a circuit of Rye Harbour Nature Reserve.

- 5.75 miles ascent 47ft descent 208 ft RATING 2...EASY/MODERATE
- 47% off road paths; 33% off road track (rural); 20% unmade/private road
- Suitable for walkers and dog walkers; there are invariably sheep grazing in sections 2,3 and 7, but I've never seen any cows on this route!
- OS Explorer Map 125 – Romney Marsh, Rye & Winchelsea
- Limited parking beside the "S" bend on Sea Road, Winchelsea which runs off the main A259 from Hastings to Rye. As the road bends sharply to the right, you will see a private road straight ahead with a 10mph speed limit and a footpath sign to Camber Castle and Rye. Park close to the hedge on the left or beside the pavement over to your right.

- Start ref: TQ 917174 Postcode: TN36 4LQ
- There are no refreshments available en route, but two friendly pubs The Bridge Inn and the New Inn in Winchelsea are both within 3 mins drive
- Websites: **www.wildrye.info; www.visitrye.co.uk; www.winchelsea.net**

Camber Castle was built by Henry VIII in 1539 to defend the threat of French and Spanish invasion. However the shallow harbour, called the Camber, soon receded and within 50 years rendered the castle largely obsolete. It is now managed by Rye Harbour Nature Reserve together with English Heritage.

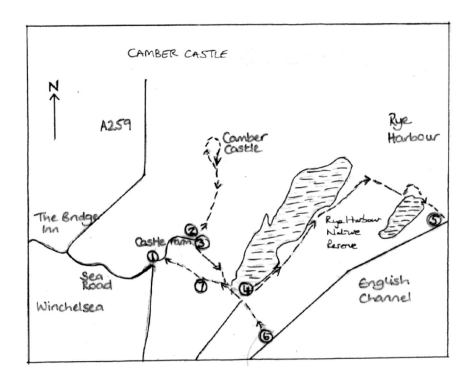

THE WALK

1. Proceed down the private road, soon passing the rescued donkeys in the field on your left! Bear round to the right and go through a gate onto a hard track with a house on your right. Over to your left you will have your first glimpse of Camber Castle. Continue along the track with farm buildings and then another house on your right until you reach **Castle Farm;** go straight ahead and cross a stile to the left of a gate which brings you into a huge open field.

2. Follow the path, partly hard track and partly grassy, directly towards **Camber Castle.** Cross over a stile to the left of the castle, and then do a circuit around the castle going over one further stile before rejoining your original path and following this back to Castle Farm.

3. After crossing the stile with **Castle Farm** ahead of you, bear left and go through a gate almost immediately on your left. Follow the path down to a gate at the bottom of the field, and join a path which soon narrows. Keep straight

Looking across at Camber Castle from the nature reserve.

ahead ignoring several left turns as the path bears round to the right with a ditch on your left. Upon reaching a junction of paths, turn left onto a wider track leading past a **gravel pit** on your left until you reach another main track junction.

4. Turn left here onto a hard/gravelled track with the gravel pit now on your left. Continue along the track for ½ mile passing several former coastguard cottages with some exotic gardens, an old boat which has seen better days and some run-down farm buildings. About ¼ mile after passing the farm buildings, take the path on your right thus leaving the main track. Within 100 yds turn right onto another track and follow this into the heart of the nature reserve. You will see small man-made lakes on either side and the **wind turbines** on Romney Marsh over to your left. Ignoring the footpath signs to your left, continue along the track as it bends its way round and you will pass a bird watching hide on your right before reaching an unmade road.

Rye Harbour Nature Reserve.

The nature reserve is a mosaic of habitats beside the sea with shingle, salt marsh, sand dunes, gravel pits, grazing marsh, reed beds and farmland. It is designated as a Site of Special Scientific Interest (SSSI) owing to the many unusual plants and animals that live there. Between late May and mid-July the wild flowers are at their colourful best, in particular the wild poppies, yellow horned poppy, viper's bugloss and red valerian. However the area is best known for its bird life and its breeding colonies, with nearly 300 species having been sighted here.

5. Turn right onto the unmade road by the information board, and continue along this for one mile....hopefully not into the teeth of a south-westerly! You will pass another hide on your right after ½ mile, and then the **Mary Stanford Lifeboat House**, a Grade II listed boathouse on your left. This commemorates the tragic loss of 17 lives from the Mary Stanford lifeboat in 1928, the biggest loss of life from a single boat in RNLI history. Slightly further along on your left hand side you will see the start of the new sea defence wall, before you take a right turn next to another information board onto a gravelled track.

Looking out across the Channel.

6. The track soon becomes softer underfoot and passes a pond down on the right before you come to the main junction of paths where you turned left at the start of section 4. This time proceed straight ahead with the gravel pit on your right, passing through one gate before reaching another path junction. Take the narrower track ahead and slightly to your left which passes between two houses and then continues to a high stile at the end of the track; ignore the turnings to your left and right.

7. Cross this stile and follow a narrow path ahead through a scrubby field until reaching a footbridge in the right hand corner. Go across the next field to the gate opposite which is often open; you can see **Castle Farm** across on your right. Continue ahead to a small footbridge, and then over a stile onto the private road that you came down at the start of the route. Turn left and you have less than 150 yds to the finish.

After completing your walk it would be practically criminal not to take the opportunity to explore the nearby towns of Winchelsea and Rye, as both are less than 5 mins drive away!

Winchelsea was probably founded originally as a Saxon fishing settlement around 800 AD. It is in a uniquely beautiful setting built on the remnants of a medieval town with its three surviving gates, the Church of St. Thomas The Martyr and its grid system, gazing out across marshland to the long since receding sea. It was once the head port of the Cinque Ports Confederation, the alliance of Kent and East Sussex ports that were a vital buffer against invasion in the days before there was a royal navy. John Wesley preached his last open air sermon in Winchelsea in 1790; the inimitable Spike Milligan is buried in the churchyard, and famous former residents include the authors Thackeray, Conrad and the actress Ellen Terry.

Rye was also an important member of the Cinque Ports Confederation in medieval times, but was better known for its smuggling activities during the 18th and 19th centuries with wool and luxury goods being the largest commodities. Rye has a well-established reputation for antique, collectors' books and record shops; art galleries; historic pubs and a veritable wealth of tea rooms amongst which I can highly recommend Hayden's Tea Rooms in the High Street!

Famous people who have lived in Rye include Spike Milligan and numerous authors including Henry James, Rumer Godden, children's author Malcolm Saville and Russell Thorndike who set his Dr. Syn novels about smuggling on the nearby Romney Marshes. Tom Chaplin, Keane's lead singer, currently lives here as do Monica and Gabriela Irimia, better known as The Cheeky Girls!

Long distance footpaths can be joined by walkers in the town. The Saxon Shore Way which starts in Gravesend, Kent and traces the coast as it was in Roman times passes through here en route to Hastings; the 1066 Country Walk starts at Pevensey and finishes at Rye; and there is also the High Weald Landscape Trail which goes all the way to Horsham.

The River Tillingham.

WALK 10: RYE

One of my favourite routes starting from the historic town of Rye, which takes you through the Tillingham Valley up towards Peasmarsh Church before dropping down through the Pelsham Estate – a hidden gem this with its own cricket ground where the West Indies and India played in the 1920s! - back across the River Tillingham and up towards Udimore. You then descend into the Brede Valley, before heading back towards Rye. Superb views all the way round!

- 8.40 miles ascent 755 ft descent 736 ft RATING 4 .... TESTING
- 58% off road paths; 19% off road hard track (rural); 21% private/unmade roads/quiet lanes; 2% main road (pavement & grass verge)
- Suitable for walkers and dog walkers; there are invariably sheep in many of the fields in sections 2, 6 and 9, but rarely any cows!
- OS Explorer Map 125 Romney Marsh, Rye & Winchelsea

- Park in the public car park behind the Kettle of Fish next to the roundabout as you approach Rye on the A259 from Winchelsea.
- Rye rail station, on the Ore - Ashford line is 5 minutes walk from the start.
- Start ref: TQ 916203 Postcode: TN33 7D
- You are spoilt for choice in terms of refreshments here, with a wide array of pubs, restaurants, tea rooms and fish & chip shops!
- Websites: **www.visitrye.co.uk**

Rye's history can be traced back to before the Norman conquest when, as a small fishing community, it was almost surrounded by water and lay within the manor of Rameslie. By the 13th century Henry III and later Edward I consolidated the defence of the realm with the charter of the Cinque Ports which meant that towns along the Kent and Sussex coast provided safe harbour. Even so Rye was almost completely destroyed by fire when the French attacked in 1377. By the 18th century its prosperity relied heavily on smuggling; hence the old vaulted cellars, secret passages and tunnels!

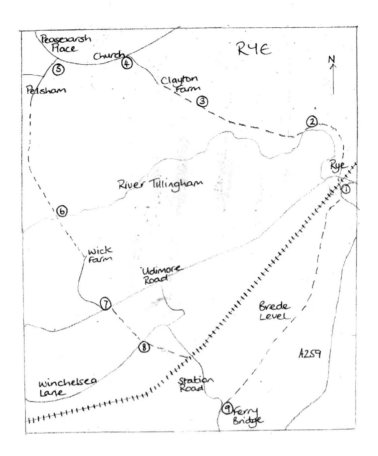

THE WALK

1. Turn right out of the car park, and immediately turn right again onto a path beside the **River Tillingham.** Go through a gate and carefully cross over the **railway line** to another gate. There has been a **windmill** on this site since the 15th century; the current model which has been built in the same style as a smock mill is a Grade 2 listed landmark, and also provides b&b accommodation! Follow the path alongside the river until reaching the **B2089 Udimore Road.** Cross over this to the stile opposite, and then follow a diagonal path across this often marshy field to a stile in the far right hand corner. Cross over this and continue along a track until going through a gate on your left hand side.

2. Follow the path along the bank with the river still on your left, until turning left before **Rolvenden Farm** which usually has the flag of St.George flying! There will be sheep grazing in most of the fields in this section. Go across the field to a stile, and then continue across the next field to a gate by the river. Go through this and bear right, continuing alongside a stream until reaching a gate by an earth bridge over another stream. You will see **Leasam House Farm** on the hillside to your right. Turn left through the gate, and then bear right as the field narrows with a stream now on your left. Continue through a gateway into the next field, which has a corrugated iron hay store on the right. Follow the path across the field to a stile at the far end. (At the time of writing the footbridge across the ditch leading to the stile had collapsed! So if the ditch is full of water, then you can go through the gate on your right and follow the bridleway signs uphill until rejoining our route through another gate halfway up the hill). Continue uphill towards a dilapidated farm building, going through one gate before the path snakes round to the right passing an old oak tree on the way to the top.

3. After passing the farm building on your right, go through the gate ahead and follow the enclosed bridleway track for nearly ¾ mile as it slowly climbs up to **Church Lane.** There are apple orchards on your right, and you will pass **Clayton Farm** halfway up.

4. Turn left onto Church Lane, and you will soon pass **St. Peter & St. Paul Church.** This is mainly Norman with a wonderful chancel, and Sir Paul McCartney's daughter Stella was married here some years ago. Both the church and Peasmarsh Place (now a residential home) stand isolated a mile from the village, so it is likely that the local community were wiped out by the plague which affected much of this area. Continue along the lane until turning left opposite **Peasmarsh Place** into **Dew Lane.**

5. Turn left as the lane sweeps round to become Starvecrow Lane, and go down the private drive towards Dew Farm. There is a bridleway sign on your right. After 450 yds turn right into the **Pelsham Estate** below. This is a gem of a discovery, right in the middle of nowhere. Nowadays the picturesque estate is mainly used for weddings and film location shoots. Incredibly its quaint cricket ground played host to the West Indies (twice) and Indian touring sides between 1928 – 1933. The great West Indies all-rounder Leary Constantine, later to become the first black man to be elected to the House of Lords, took two wickets in the 1928 against HDG Leveson-Gower's XI. All three matches were drawn by the way.

The Pelsham Estate.

Follow the drive for 600 yds through the middle of the estate, passing a large duck pond where I have sometimes seen kingfishers (a rare treat!) and the cricket ground with its own pavilion. After passing **Pelsham Farm** on your right, bear right onto a bridleway track leading uphill. The enclosed track levels off briefly at the top before dropping downhill giving you superb views of the Tillingham Valley. Go through two gates and then cross a footbridge over the **River Tillingham.**

6. Go straight across the next two fields before climbing up a very steep hill to a gate at the top. **Wick Farm** is across on your left. Follow the path for a short distance before turning right onto a private drive, still following the bridleway signs. Continue along the drive which gradually climbs uphill for 650 yds until reaching the **B2089 Udimore Road.**

7. Turn left onto the main road, and take great care crossing over to the grass verge opposite. Continue for 200 yds before turning right immediately after **Woodside Cottage** onto a path through a short stretch of woodland. Follow the path to a stile, from where you have a magnificent view over the Brede Valley; in the distance you can see Sir Paul McCartney's windmill at Icklesham and Fairlight Church, Winchelsea is straight ahead and across to your left the wind turbines on Romney Marsh.

The view from Udimore into the Brede valley.

Go diagonally across the field to a stile and across a short strip to the next stile. Cross over into a huge crop field, and continue ahead for 100 yds before bearing right close to a pylon and dropping sharply downhill towards a lane. Go over two stiles in quick succession at the bottom, leading onto **Winchelsea Lane.**

8. Cross over the footbridge slightly to your left, and head diagonally across the field to an earth bridge leading into the next field. Aim for the top left hand corner of this field, and go through a gap onto **Winchelsea Lane.** Turn right and take great care going over the level crossing; **Winchelsea station** is on your right. Continue along **Station Road** for 750 yds until reaching a footpath sign just before **Ferry Bridge** which goes over the River Brede. You now have just 1.75 miles to go!

9. You will soon see the town of **Rye** in the distance, dominated by St. Mary's Church, and basically you are aiming for the windmill next to the start. Cross the stile and head diagonally across the field to enter a much larger field. Go across this field to a footbridge, and then aim for the top left hand corner of the next field where you then follow alongside a stream – **the Padiam Sewer** – for a short distance before crossing a footbridge on your left. Turn right and follow the raised path across the centre of the next two fields linked by more footbridges, until going over a stile into a large field. Follow the path beside the stream, going through a number of gates, until reaching a hard track which leads out past a farm building and several houses onto the **A259.** Turn left onto the pavement, and the finish is just 150 yds away.

Great Dixter.

WALK 11: NORTHIAM

An extremely scenic route of nearly 3.50 miles with some lovely views, particularly in the early stages, as you follow the Sussex Border Path from Great Dixter out towards Ewhurst. You should also take the opportunity to visit the lovely gardens at Great Dixter, originally laid out by Lutyens.

- 3.33 miles ascent 405 ft descent 408 ft RATING 1 ..... EASY
- 75% off road paths; 1% off road hard track (rural); 24% quiet lanes
- Suitable for walkers and dog walkers; there are usually sheep in some of the fields in sections 1,2 and 5, although rarely any cows!
- OS Explorer map 125 Romney Marsh, Rye & Winchelsea
- Park in either of the car parks at Great Dixter which is at the far end of Dixter Lane, ½ mile from the A28 which runs through Northiam
- Start ref: TQ 819251 Postcode: TN31 6PH
- Refreshments are available at the Hayes Inn, a very historic pub on the village

green, which is at the halfway mark of the route. There is also a small tea-rooms, Pat-A-Cake Bakers, on the opposite side of the green
• Websites: **www.greatdixter.co.uk**

Northiam dates back to Anglo-Saxon times with "hiam" meaning water meadow where hay grows. Great Dixter is a series of wonderful gardens arranged around a 15th century Grade 1 listed medieval timber framed house. The gardening writer Christopher Lloyd who transformed these gardens, one of the best loved in the South East, died in 2006 but their future is secure now thanks to lottery funding.

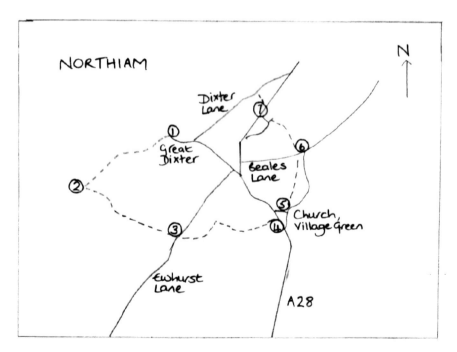

THE WALK

1. Starting at the foot of the drive just beyond Great Dixter, cross over a stile to the left of a cattle grid pointing to Ewhurst. You are now on the **Sussex Border Path.** Follow the path which bears round to the left, keeping a hedge on your left hand side. Cross over the next stile/gate with a pond on your right, and enjoy some wonderful views towards Ewhurst as you head diagonally downhill to a small stile which takes you into the next field. Go straight across this field which drops downhill to a footbridge over a stream.

2. After crossing the footbridge turn left, and follow the path beside the stream which soon passes through a small copse into the next field. Go straight across this field to a footbridge which leads into another field. Within 200 yds bear left into a gateway and cross the stile/gate into the next field. Bear right and, keeping the line of trees on your right, make your way across the field to a stile which leads onto **Ewhurst Lane.**

3. Cross over the lane into a private driveway, and almost immediately bear left up a path which runs alongside the entrance to **Strawberry Hole Cottage.** Cross over the stile at the end of this short path, and continue uphill across the field to the next stile which is to the right of a small copse. After crossing the stile you then head uphill towards the recreation ground, but turn right along a path just before the brow of the hill. Follow the path as it heads in the direction of **St. Mary's Church,** dropping briefly downhill to a footbridge which leads you into another field. Follow the path with a hedge on your right, which then joins a gravelled drive in between houses leading up to the **A28.**

4. Cross over the main road to the opposite pavement, bearing left by the village green into **Church Lane** where you now leave the Sussex Border Path. You will see a time-battered oak tree with a plaque denoting that the young Queen Elizabeth I stopped off here in 1573 on her way to Rye, and enjoyed a meal at this very spot made by George Bishop and family from Hayes Farm. There is a pleasant garden to the rear of the Hayes Inn, whilst on the opposite side of the road is Pat-A-Cake bakers and tea-rooms. Continue along Church Lane passing **St. Mary's Church** on your right which dates back to 1090.

71

5. Shortly after passing the church turn left into **Fullers Lane,** and go through a gate immediately on your right with a sign pointing to Goddens Gill. Cross this field which invariably has sheep in, keeping the hedge to your right until reaching a gate which takes you into the next field. As you head downhill enjoy the countryside views before climbing slightly to reach the next gate. You will see a sand school for horses on your right as you follow the path to a gate leading onto **Beales Lane.**

6. Cross over this narrow lane with a pretty, thatched farmhouse **Wildings Farm** ahead of you. Slightly to your right you will see an unusual gate which opens above a stone wall. Follow the path to **Goddens Gill** going downhill between post and rail fenced fields with horses in, until reaching the delightfully named **Harlot's Wood!** This short section of woodland path can become quite greasy in wet conditions. After crossing a small footbridge follow the path uphill until reaching the end of a residential cul-de-sac, with some lock-up garages on your left. Bear right as you approach a large green, and this quickly

The famous oak tree on the village green at Northiam.

brings you out to the **A28.**

7. Cross over the main road to the opposite pavement, and within a few yards turn left through a gate into a small reserve **Knelle View** with a pond on your right. Follow the path as it snakes its way up between two houses to emerge on **Dixter Lane.** Turn left and continue along the lane for circa ½ mile, ignoring a left turn Beacon Lane. Just before you reach the turning to Great Dixter, enjoy the splendid views on your right towards **Bodiam,** before continuing down the enclosed driveway to the finish.

Bodiam Castle.

WALK 12: BODIAM

A very scenic route of nearly 6 miles starting from picturesque Bodiam Castle, one of the National Trust's crown jewels!

- 5.75 miles ascent 506 ft descent 508 ft RATING 3 ...MODERATE
- 54% off road paths; 30% off road hard track (rural); 16% quiet lanes
- Suitable for walkers and dog walkers; there are sometimes sheep and cows on one field in section 2, but otherwise a livestock free route!
- OS Explorer Map 136 – High Weald
- Park either in the National Trust car park at Bodiam Castle, or on the opposite side of the road near The Castle pub
- Start ref: TQ 785256 Postcode: TN32 5UA
- Refreshments are available in the National Trust tea rooms in the Castle car park, and also at the Castle Inn, which is a very historic pub and was once the only hostelry in England to be actually owned by Guinness being in the centre

of a large hop-growing area! I can vouch for the excellent menu here, especially the desserts!, and there is a river terrace with a great view over the River Rother
- Websites: **www.nationaltrust.org.uk/bodiamcastle**

Bodiam Castle, maintained by the National Trust, was begun in 1385 and is remarkably well preserved. Mounted ramparts allow you to view the fortress in its superb setting in the Rother Valley. The castle was built for the Sussex knight Sir Edward Dalyngrigge who was prominent in the 100 Years War, and was given a licence to build by the grateful monarch Richard II. The walls of this seemingly impregnable castle are circa 6.5 feet thick, but apart from a minor skirmish in 1484 have never witnessed a siege! Bodiam itself was originally a port and main crossing point from Battle to North Kent, and in the last century was also an important hop-growing area.

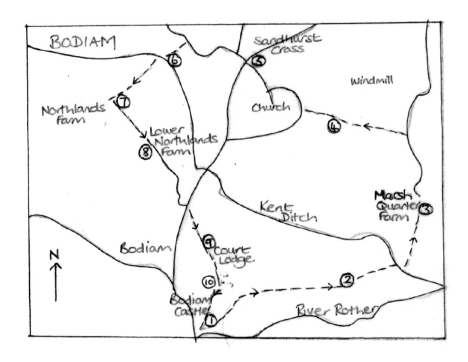

THE WALK

1. Starting at the information board in the castle car park, go through the gate behind this and follow the hard track which sweeps round towards the castle before bearing right to exit the castle grounds through a gate next to a cattle grid. Continue along the track for a mile, which runs parallel to the **River Rother** which is several fields away on your right hand side.

2. After ¾ mile you will pass a solitary house on your left, and at the end of the track cross over a footbridge which straddles the **Kent Ditch;** this marks the **Kent/East Sussex border.** There is a pumping station on your right. After crossing the bridge go down the bank ahead of you and slightly to your right, which then drops down into a field the other side. Bear left at the bottom of the bank, and follow the path beside a small ditch dividing two fields to a footbridge opposite which also crosses another ditch. On entering this field head slightly uphill towards the next stile/gate opposite (the gate is often left open), and follow the path in the next field past a pylon and up to a gate to the left of

76

Going along the Rother Valley towards the Kent Ditch.

Marsh Quarter Farm. Dog walkers please note that this last field is often occupied by sheep and sometimes cows.

3. After passing through the gate with the farmhouse to your right, you will quickly join an unmade road/hard track **Marsh Quarter Lane** which sweeps round to the right past a pond before heading gradually uphill. Shortly after passing **Little Marsh Quarter** on your right, take a path on your left through an open field. The stone marker here is often hidden by vegetation. Follow the path to a stile in the middle of a copse. After crossing the stile, bear right and follow the narrow path which leads you into another field. Go straight across this field to the stile opposite, from where you will have lovely views of the surrounding countryside.

4. Follow the path diagonally across to your right to the next stile, and you will have a splendid view of **St. Nicholas Church** at Sandhurst Cross. Over to your right you can see the **Sandhurst windmill,** which is believed to be the only five sweep smock mill in the South East. Originally built in 1844 it was last worked in 1912, but has now been reconstructed after being dismantled in the early 1950s for safety reasons.

The windmill at Sandhurst.

The path across this field leads to a stile/gate which brings you out onto a narrow private road with the church up ahead of you. Turn right onto the road, and you have a short, but stiff climb until reaching the church on your left. The church was completed by the time of the Black Death in the mid 14th century, and is some distance away from the main village probably owing to the number of plague victims buried in the churchyard. The private road joins **Church Road** and leads you past some pretty houses and cottages to the junction with **Bodiam Road.**

5. Cross over Bodiam Road, taking great care as the traffic can be quite fast at this point, into **Silverden Lane,** and within 100 yds bear left onto a narrow lane **Bourne Lane.** You can enjoy some great views across to your left as the lane winds its way down past several houses before becoming more of a track. Just before the track levels off at the bottom, go over a stile on your left which is opposite a copse, and follow the path beside the stream which can often be quite boggy in wet weather. This field is in the process of being converted to hop-growing.

Great views from Bourne Lane across to Northlands Farm.

6. Just before the end of the field cross an earth bridge on your right over the stream – the ubiquitous **Kent Ditch!** Bear left and within another 100 yds cross a footbridge over the Kent Ditch again. Go straight across the field to another earth bridge (your final encounter with the Kent Ditch!) and you then begin a steady climb with some woods on your right. After passing a small copse on your left, continue ahead along a track leading to **Northlands Farm.**

7. Just before reaching Northlands Farm, turn left onto a grassy path and enjoy a nice downhill stretch leading into some woods. Cross the earth bridge at the bottom over a stream, and go over the stile in front of you. A short uphill section between fenced in fields leads you onto a track with a house on your right. At the end of the track is a gate which passes through **Lower Northlands Farm** onto a narrow lane.

8. Continue along this lane with hop fields on your left hand side for 600 yds until reaching the junction with **Bodiam Road.** Cross over and within 20 yds turn left into an open field which has a footpath marker on the right (sometimes hidden by vegetation). You then have a tough uphill climb diagonally across to a stile at the top.

9. Bear left over the stile, and within 100 yds cross over the next stile. Follow the path for a short distance before scrambling up a steep bank on your right to another stile. Cross over the narrow private driveway to Court Lodge Farm and go across the grassy bank ahead of you; the impressive **Court Lodge** is on your right with it's pig, cow and horse weathervanes! Bear left through an open gateway and you will see a large open schooling area for horses in front of you. Turn right here, keeping a fence on your right, and you are then greeted by a quite superb view of **Bodiam Castle** as you follow the path downhill with a vineyard on your right until reaching a stile at the bottom.

10. Cross the stile, and then bear right across the grass in front of the castle until reaching the track. Follow the track with the castle on your left, and then bear right after passing the castle and head for the car park entrance.

The descent to Bodiam Castle.

A superb view from St. George Church, Brede.

WALK 13: BREDE

A very scenic route of nearly 6 miles with superb views of the Brede Valley, passing by historic Brede Place before crossing over into the Tillingham Valley and following the river Tillingham towards Beckley Furnace. You then face a testing climb towards Broad Oak, before an easy last mile across country enjoying great views stretching all the way to Fairlight.

- 5.85 miles ascent 757 ft descent 773 ft RATING 4........TESTING
- 69% off road paths; 10% off road hard track (rural); 18% private/unmade roads/quiet lanes; 3% main road (pavement)
- Suitable for walkers and dog walkers; however there are sheep present in many of the fields en route, and sometimes cows in one field as you enter the Tillingham Valley
- OS Explorer Map 124 Hastings & Bexhill
- Park in Stubb Lane opposite the scout hut. Brede is on the A28 Hastings to

Ashford road; turn right immediately after passing The Red Lion at the top of Brede Hill into a narrow lane (unnamed) which quickly joins Stubb Lane. Turn right and park where you can.

- Start ref: TQ 823187 Postcode: TN31 6EJ
- Refreshments are available at The Red Lion nearby, which also has a garden at the rear of the pub
- Websites: **www.1066country.com**

Brede was first mentioned in a charter from the time of King Canute in the early 11th century, and its name was probably derived from the Anglo-Saxon "Braed" meaning broad which described the sea estuary out towards Westfield. It was famous for its iron works and produced cannon and shot until the late 1770s when gunpowder was manufactured. In 1808 Brede Gunpowder Mills was completely destroyed by a large explosion. St.George Church was built by Benedictine monks from Fecamp Abbey in Normandy around 1180; the manor of Brede was controlled by the Abbey from 1030 - 1416.

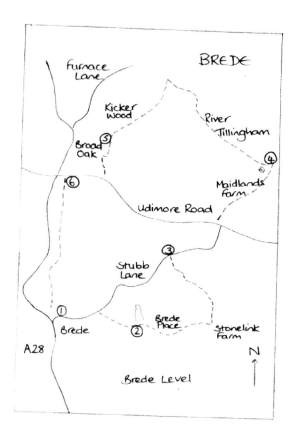

THE WALK

1. Proceed down **Stubb Lane** for 400 yds, and just after passing the speed limit signs turn right onto a path which leads through woodland and across a private drive to a gate. Head diagonally down across the field to a gate in the bottom left hand corner, with wonderful views across the Brede Valley. Go through the gate into the next field, and follow the path down towards another gate at the bottom. Go straight ahead onto a private drive, turning left by **Hare Farm** opposite and along the drive to a stile beside the gate. You have a great view from there of a lake and **Brede Place** which has a fascinating history. A 14th century stone manor house built by one of Edward III's knights, it was owned by the Oxenbridge family who had close links with Queen Elizabeth I for 250 years. It was bought by Sir Edward Frewen in 1708 and has remained in the family ever since! However for much of the 18th and part of the 19th centuries the old house became so dilapidated that it was uninhabitable, and was used by smugglers to store contraband goods. The Frewens returned to their home at the beginning of the 20th century, and Moreton Frewen continued the restoration work which had started in the 1870s. Moreton, who inherited the house, was a handsome charmer who spent most of his time in America. He was known as a racecourse gambler and in his wild aspirations to make a fortune, such were his disasters that he earned the nickname "Mortal Ruin!" However he was always able to use his family connections and later married into wealthy US society.

A steep climb as you pass beside Brede Place.

2. Go over the stile to a footbridge, where you then face a steepling climb (pictured above) which gives you plenty of time to admire the views! Go through the gate at the top of the field, and then across a private drive to another gate opposite. Head diagonally left across this field to a gap in the hedgerow, and continue downhill across the next field to a rickety stile at the bottom. As you cross the stile the next piece of ground is invariably boggy, so try and skirt round the edge of this as you scramble up a steep bank to a very high stile. For dog walkers who can't get their beasts over this stile, there is a gate 50 yds to your right which leads into the next paddock! Go across the paddock to a gate which leads onto a private drive to **Stonelink Farm** on your right. Turn left and proceed for 300 yds along the drive. After passing **Peasridge** bear left across a grassy area down to a well hidden stile at the edge of a wood. A short path leads you down into a ditch and then into an open field. The path across this field can be difficult to follow, but basically you need to head diagonally across to the top right corner of the field. After passing a farmhouse on your right, you will then stumble across another well hidden stile another 100 yds further along on your right; you can see the private drive to **Brede Place** down to your left. Cross over the stile, and then go over another two stiles as the path wends its way beside a wood until coming to a grassy area with a field on your right. Go diagonally across the grass to the private drive; turn right and within 100 yds exit through the main gates onto **Stubb Lane.**

3. Turn right onto this quiet lane, and follow it for nearly ½ mile until its junction with **Udimore Road.** Take care crossing this road with the fast moving traffic, and turn into the track opposite leading to **Maidland's Farm.** Follow the track for 600 yds, ignoring the track on your right to **Maidlands Oast.** Just after passing the oasthouse, the track runs out in an open field. You have some great views over to your right as far as the wind turbines on Romney Marsh and Dungeness. Follow a path across the field, with a house on your left, to a gate at the bottom. As you enter the next field you are greeted by superb views of the Tillingham Valley; head downhill across the centre of the field to a stile by the left of a copse. On entering this field, the footpath splits.

4. Bear left to join the path along the line of the **river Tillingham,** following this past the small lake to a footbridge. Dog walkers note that there are sometimes cows in this field. You have now reached the halfway point of the route. Cross the footbridge, and continue across the next three fields which are also linked by footbridges , keeping the river on your right. As you leave the last field go through a gate onto a private driveway, and bear left by a wooden bungalow onto an unmade road. Not far from here was the site of the **Beckley Furnace,** which closed in the 1770s. Follow the road uphill for 300 yds before going through a gate into a field; go across the field to a stile which leads into a much larger field. You have another steep climb in store, heading diagonally across to a gate in the top right hand corner of the field, keeping **Kicker Wood** on your right hand side. Go through the gate onto a track, then bear right heading uphill to a gate which leads you into a field from where you can see a

Glorious views in the Tillingham Valley.

residential estate.

5. Follow the path on the left hand side of the field to a gate, and then follow the path between houses leading onto a residential cul-de-sac. Turn right and within 50 yds turn left into another cul-de-sac **The Martlets.** Follow the drive at the end which leads to a BT station, and take the path on the left which quickly brings you out onto the main **Udimore Road.** Turn right and then take care crossing over to the opposite pavement, continuing for 350 yds towards the **Broad Oak** junction with the A28 passing **Brede Methodist Church** and **Brede Primary School.** Immediately after passing a bus stop, turn left by the footpath sign.

6. Cross the stile at end of the short path which joins up with the driveway for **Sunbeam Farm.** Continue straight ahead, passing farm buildings on your right and follow the path across a narrow field to a stile. Go across this and follow the path downhill to a gate which leads into a small wood. After going through a gate at the other end of the wood, bear right and you will soon see a large pond on your right. Bear left here, and follow the path past a large tree towards a gate halfway across this large field. Go through the gate onto an enclosed path with a hedgerow on your left and gardens on your right. Follow this path for some way until reaching a stile leading into a field. Cross the stile and then aim for a gap to the right of a large tree, which leads you into the next field, and continue across this to a gate in the top right hand corner. Having gone through the gate, then turn left onto the path in this next field form where you have splendid views all the way across towards Fairlight. Follow the path to the gate at the bottom. Go through this, and follow the path downhill which peters out to a narrow path between houses leading onto the **A28.** Turn left onto the pavement, and then almost immediately left again into **Stubb Lane** and back to the start.

The village green at Sedlescombe.

WALK 14: SEDLESCOMBE

A very enjoyable route of just over 6 miles, with some great views of Westfield, following the 1066 Country Walk for much of the middle section going out across Kent Street and briefly crossing Sedlescombe Golf Course into Battle Great Wood.

● 6.10 miles ascent 528 ft descent 587 ft RATING 3......MODERATE
● 57% off road paths; 14% off road track (rural); 26% private/unmade roads/ quiet lanes; 3% main road (pavement).
● Suitable for walkers and dog walkers; this is a relatively livestock free route with just a handful of fields in section 2 which sometimes contain cows and some fields in section 3 which usually have sheep grazing. Please note that much of the section 4 between Spraysbridge and Kent Street is invariably very slippery after it's been raining, and can be very boggy during winter.
● OS Explorer Map 124 Hastings & Bexhill.

- Parking is readily available, either next to the village green or in the main village car park, 100 yds on the right past the Brickwall Hotel in Brede Lane. Sedlescombe lies on the B2244, which runs off the A21 from Hastings
- Start ref: TQ 781180 Postcode: TN33 OQA
- Refreshments are available either at The Queen's Head, a traditional pub on the village green, or at the Clockhouse Bistro opposite the green.
- Websites: **www.1066country.com**

Sedlescombe, which won the Calor East Sussex Village of the Year in 2009, traces its routes back to Roman times. Indeed the oldest house in the village, Asselton House which is on the village green, was formerly called Asselton Bath and is reputed to be on the site of a Roman bathhouse. The area was used for many years for the manufacture of explosives, and both the river Brede and its tributary the river Line flow through it. Pestalozzi International Children's Village, an educational charity set up for children from developing countries to live and study, was established during the Second World War and lies at the southern end of the village.

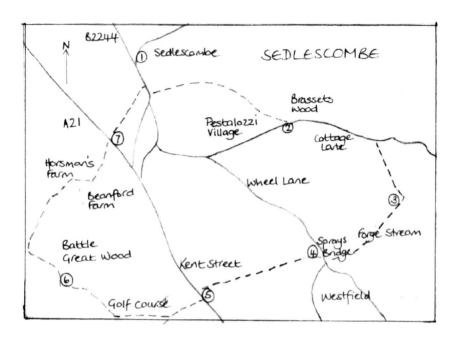

THE WALK

1. Passing the **Queen's Head** on your left, continue downhill for 300 yds past some very pleasant and historic houses on your left and the village green on your right. After crossing Sedlescombe Bridge over the **river Brede,** turn left through a gate into playing fields; you will see **Pestalozzi Children's Village** across to your right. Continue alongside the river across the playing fields to a gate; go through this and follow the path through a gap into the next field with the river still to your left. Within another 100 yds go over the stile on your right, then bear left across the field to a large metal gate. The path leads into a much larger field where, ignoring the footpath sign to your left, continue straight across the field to a stile leading into a small wood. Cross this and follow the windy path, watching out for the many tree roots!, through woodland to another stile which brings you into a large field. Bear left, and the path soon joins a larger track which runs through the centre of the field before climbing sharply uphill towards a gate at the edge of **Brasset's Wood.** Cross over a track to the path ahead, and after 200 yds exit the wood by a footpath sign onto **Cottage Lane** opposite **The Lodge nursery.**

2. Turn left onto the lane and continue for 800 yds before turning right onto a woodland path opposite a telegraph pole; you will see a stone footpath marker.

This leads into a field with a pylon on your right. Go ahead to a stile from where you have the most superb view down into the valley of Westfield and The Ridge beyond. As you step down into the next field you will have to duck under some electric fencing, before heading downhill.

View over Westfield as you head downhill to Forge Stream.

This field and the next smaller field do sometimes have cows in. Cross a stile into the smaller field, and then in quick succession a stile and footbridge over **Forge Stream.**

3. Bear right after crossing the footbridge, and follow the path beside the stream to a large gate. Go across the centre of the next field to another large gate, and continue for 150 yds before crossing a footbridge on your right. Here you will join the 1066 Country Walk path, which will take you all the way into Battle Great Wood. Follow the path to a stile which leads into a large field with a marshy area on your left....in the spring you may well hear the unmistakeable call of the marsh frog! Continue across the field to a footbridge which brings you out at **Spraysbridge** on **Wheel Lane.** Immediately opposite is

Spraysbridge Farm, a Grade 2 listed Wealden farmhouse built in 1691, which stands on the edge of an old Roman road leading from the site of iron ore workings on Platnix Farm to Sedlescombe. Turn right over the bridge, and in 50 yds cross the stile on your left by the footpath marker Battle 2.5 miles.

4. Cross the stile and then aim for the top of the bank on your right, where you will see another footpath marker. Follow the path as it crosses over a stile and leads to a footbridge into the next field. Go across this field and then through a gateway into the next field, where you exit in the bottom left corner. Bear right and follow the path over a footbridge leading into a long, narrow field with fenced in woodland (often containing free range pigs!) on your left and Forge Stream on your right. Continue across the field until crossing a farm track with a pond to your right, then aim for a small gate directly ahead. Follow the woodland path as it crosses over a footbridge, and leads up to a small gate opening out into a large field. Go across the centre of the field to a stile, and then follow an enclosed path between back gardens to a gate which brings you out onto the **A21.**

5. Take great care crossing this extremely busy road to the entrance opposite to **Sedlescombe Golf Club.** Turn left and go 50 yds past the entrance along the grass verge, before picking up the 1066 Country Walk signs once again directing you onto a private road leading to **Nortons Farm.** Follow this for 400 yds passing The Oasthouse and Nortons Farm on your left. Go through a large metal gate at the end of this road, and follow the path for 150 yds until reaching a gate which leads onto the golf course. Go across to join the hard track 50 yds ahead which leads through the centre of the course, looking out for low flying golf balls! After 400 yds turn right at the end of the track, and within 50 yds turn left onto a woodland path at the edge of **Battle Great Wood.** This drops downhill and can become very greasy further along after it's been raining. Turn left at the bottom as the path joins a much larger track, and within 50 yds turn right at a main junction of tracks. You are now leaving the 1066 Country Walk path. The Forestry Commission operated Great Wood consists of coniferous woodland, with areas of heathland, ponds, streams and sweet chestnut coppice, and is home to a wealth of wildlife including deer.

6. Follow the hard track for 400 yds as it gradually climbs uphill before levelling off. As the track begins to swing round to the left, continue straight ahead along a much narrower path which soon brings you into a narrow strip

Battle Great Wood.

with woodland on either side. Turn right and follow the path all the way to a gate on the edge of woodland. Go through the gate and follow the path which descends gently to a tall gate enclosed by high wooden fencing. Go through the gate, and within 50 yds turn left through a gate onto a hard track. Follow this past **Horsmans Farm** on your left for 400 yds all the way down to the **A21**. Again take great care crossing this very busy road to the stile opposite, where you will see a footpath marker for Sedlescombe.

7. Cross the stile and follow the path downhill across the field to a footbridge. Follow the well marked path over 5 footbridges in quick succession, which will lead you out past a small recreation ground and onto the **B2244** at the southern end of **Sedlescombe**. Cross the road, and head uphill past the village green to the finish.

The Author

Nick Brown

Being a keen runner and walker, it has been a longstanding ambition of mine to compile a book of some of my favourite off road routes in the 1066 area. I first started exploring the surrounding countryside after moving down from London in 1986, and am still constantly amazed by the sheer beauty and variety of scenery which is on our doorstep. I sincerely hope that you will get as much pleasure from these routes as I have over the years, and look forward to receiving your comments on the website **www.spanglefish.com/1066routes** .

Nick Brown lives at Westfield, just outside Hastings, and is a member of both Hastings Runners and Dulwich Runners. Aged 52, he has been running competitively and walking for nearly 25 years. He won the local Beckley 10kms in both 2005 and 2006, the East Sussex Sunday Cross Country League (M40 category) in 2006/2007, and has finished in the top 50 of the Hastings half marathon (voted the most popular in the UK) on a number of occasions. As well as exploring the 1066 area, he has also walked extensively in both Switzerland and Normandy.

Walking South East

Walking South East is the brand name for the walking publications produced by Trailguides that cover the south eastern counties of England.

Being a small independent publisher Trailguides specialises in the small, local guide written by the local author. To us this produces a guide that is user-friendly, easy to use and provides as much information as possible and all in an easily readable format. In essence, to increase the enjoyment of the walker and to showcase the very best of our landscape.

Our series of books explores the heritage of us all and lets you see your region with new eyes. These books are written to not juts take you on a walk but to investigate, explore and understand the objects, places and history that has shaped not just the countryside but also the people of this corner of England.

If you've enjoyed following the routes in this guide and want news and details of other publications that are being developed under the Walking South East label then look at the company website at **www.trailguides.co.uk**

Comments and, yes, criticisms, are always welcomed especially if you discover a change to a route. Contact us by email through the website or by post at Trailguides Limited, 35 Carmel Road South, Darlington, Co Durham DL3 8DQ.

Other walking books from Walking South East.
At the time of publication the following books are available but with new titles being regularly added to our publication list keep checking our website.

East Sussex.
Walks in 1066 Country.

Acknowledgements

Firstly I would like to thank my partner Helen Brown for her support and encouragement, and for accompanying me on some of the shorter routes which we usually ran round. During the course of compiling this book, we must have visited practically all the tea rooms in the area. Then a special thanks to my best friend Martin Noakes who accompanied me on some of the longer routes. Also a word of thanks to Helen's oldest son Thomas, who helped set up my website. Many thanks also to Westfield artist Lorraine Ashley for her superb map of the walks and to Bexhill artist Karin Woolstencroft who patiently hand drew all the route maps. Many thanks to Cliff Braybrooke of the Battle Historical Society, who gave me some helpful information for Walk 3 Battle. And finally a massive thank you to Guy Selmon and the orthopaedic team at The Conquest Hospital in Hastings, whose expertise has enabled me to recover from a serious lower back problem and resume my outdoor activities !

Disclaimer

Back cover: The view from St. Nicholas Church at Sandhurst Cross - **Walk 12** Bodiam.
Main picture: The wooded track at Snaylham - **Walk 7** Guestling.

The 1066 area is one of the most beautiful in the South East, and absolutely steeped in history. Yet to many people 1066 simply means the Battle of Hastings, Battle Abbey and all that, and they are quite unaware of the superb scenery throughout the area.

Picturesque towns, quaint hamlets, magnificent castles, Anglo-Saxon and Norman churches, oast houses, windmills, ancient woodland, rivers, stunning valleys and cliff top paths....hard to believe that all this is contained within a relatively small area, just waiting to be explored!

In this series of 14 walks, the author uses his considerable local knowledge to offer a rich choice of routes spread across 1066 Country which should enable you to enjoy this magnificent countryside at its very best!

35 Carmel Road South
Darlington, County Durham
DL3 8DQ
www.trailguides.co.uk

ISBN 978-1-905444-39-7

£10.99